Like Son

Like Son

Runner on the Bridge Publishing

first edition / January 2019

All rights reserved

Copyright © 2019 by Alexander Sebastian

www.runneronthebridge.com

No part of this publication may be reproduced, stored or transmitted in any form or by any means, electronic, mechanical, photocopying, recording, scanning, or otherwise without written permission from the publisher. It is illegal to copy this book, post it to a website, or distribute it by any other means without permission

ISBN: 978-0-578-43672-2

For Blanca Aurora Guzman

On the Beach

It wasn't about the money. Even back then, five dollars wasn't a lot.

"To the end of the beach and back. You getta head start." Him, forty-nine years old, fit, white tennis shorts, white T-shirt with a red collar, white hair. Me, ten years old, brown curly hair and a bit of a belly, blue corduroy shorts. Both of us barefoot. An early morning fog sat on the Monterey coast. It was just us and the seagulls.

"On your mark . . . go!" He took off in a sprint, ignoring his own suggestion of a head start for me. He thought it was hilarious, hoping the funny trick would throw me off, but I wasn't playing around.

A burst of adrenaline quickly got me twenty yards ahead, but knowing nothing about pacing, my working lungs started to slow me down before the turnaround. I was told I was born with small lungs, though I don't know how anyone knew that for sure. I could sense him behind me, sizing me up as my feet sunk into the wet sand. When I turned 180 degrees to catch a look, he was closer than I thought. Soon after, he passed me with a don't-forget-who's-boss smile. No one had taught me yet about negative splits.

Now I was mad. When he overtook me I went from leader to chaser. And I was chasing my grandfather. A new motivation filled me. I didn't care about the money, the tingling in my chest, the heavy legs. All I wanted to do was beat him. Something beyond me, which I had yet to recognize, kept me on his tail when I was past the point of fatigue. He may have had more endurance at his age, but I believed I could best him with my raw kid speed if I could just stay close enough to tap into it at the end. I started to see stars. I wondered if the seagulls were yelling at me. The finish line seemed to be moving away from me faster than I could reach it. But as I started to reel him back in, I tapped into that hunger for a win that felt beyond me. I passed him back and collapsed in victory beyond the finish line we had drawn on the beach, spent and satisfied. I lay on my back on the cold sand, chest heaving, staring up at the gray sky.

"I beat you," I said between big breaths. He didn't respond but I knew he wasn't upset. There was no one else in the world I wanted to beat more than my grandfather. It's curious to me now—not being a competitive person—that I made the man who introduced me to distance running, a man I came to love, the most important opponent in my childhood. Beating him in anything became an itch that had to be scratched.

Still breathing hard, I wanted to make it official.

"When do I get my money?"

He laughed. He loved it all.

"Some day," he said with a laugh. "When you're big and strong like me."

Bay to Breakers

"Do you call yourself a runner?"

Sometimes the running is about unfinished business. And so it was when I returned to the Bay to Breakers 12K after a twenty-eight year break. I was an earnest thirteen-year-old kid back in 1982, trying my best to run my first race. Now I was a forty-one-year-old who was trying to earn back the right to call himself a "runner." I had resisted the event because I didn't want to jog with the crowds. I had disdain for the yahoos mocking something I took so seriously now. Nothing felt lighthearted about how hard I wanted to run.

When someone asks me when I started running, I proudly tell them I ran the Bay to Breakers when I was thirteen. For that early start, I have my grandfather to thank. Running in the morning around the neighborhood, racing down the beach, or contesting at the local track for some simple wager of cash or a car washing, there was never any hard pressure from him. Yet, it was competition. Fun, yes, and undoubtedly a race. That strong and giving man offered me an enduring gift that I will never be able to thank him enough for. If he only knew how much the gift of running would change my life, how his early morning invitations to run with him would transfer some of his strength to me. He has always been generous with the things he loves.

He suggested we run the Bay to Breakers. He first ran it in the early seventies, when finisher certificates were completed by hand by the race director. Seven and a half miles? Sure. "But we'll have to train," he warned. Ok. Every other morning I got up on my own to run three miles before school. My friends could hardly run around the block, making this endeavor the beginning of defining myself among my peers as a runner. At thirteen I thought that was cool. I felt lucky to have an identity, something I could call my own.

But the race didn't go as we had planned. Though I was ready to cover the distance, fifty thousand runners with the same plan made anything more than a shuffle physically impossible. As is the absurdity of all Bay to Breakers, we crossed the start line as the winner, Rod Dixon, crossed the finish line in 35:08. And we continued to walk, past miles one, two, three, and up Hayes Hill. We'd have gaps where we thought, *Ok, now we can go*, only to find ourselves stifled by yet another roadside attraction, floats and snakes and costumes better suited for a parade. With enough space to finally run in the panhandle of Golden Gate Park, I ran out of anger a mere three miles from the finish. My grandfather withheld hollow praise, running silently in my shadow. I felt released, flying down JFK Drive, fantasizing about being on the evening news while I ran strong to make my grandfather proud.

But at the finish line, all I remember is feeling disappointment that I wouldn't be able to tell everyone I ran the whole way. I was frustrated, questioning what all the work was for, feeling like I wasn't really a runner since I didn't cover the distance. I didn't prove anything to anyone. At home my grandmother told me, not for the first time, that I was being too hard on myself. But I didn't really know what she meant. I crossed the event off my list and left it and running behind for a long time. I was a kid. Kids are good at moving on.

When I spontaneously took up running again in 2005, my goals were very pedestrian—to shed some pounds and get in shape. A common story. I ran every day. But as I kept at it, my long runs became my daily runs. I was thrilled by racing. My life started to revolve around marathon training cycles. Slowly, I had become a runner again.

As I lined up at the 2010 Bay to Breakers, I wanted two things. First, I wanted it to be the end release of a bad work week, the kind that makes you bring home the running outfit you had planned on using after work, unused. I would use this race to remind myself I was a runner at heart, if not by trade, and not the worker bee I obligated myself to be.

Second, I asked the race to be an end chapter to an unfocused half year when my running stagnated. I'd had life-changing races in Seattle (Boston qualifier), Boston (Boston Marathon!), and New York (top of the tops). I was ready for the next step, to bring to a close my drawn-out transformation into a decent athlete and to see what possible meaning lurked beyond the simple act of running. Since I left that 1982 Bay to Breakers with something still to prove, it seemed fitting to return to make matters right. End points also make good starting points.

In 1982, the start gun meant nothing more than a sea swell of the crowd, a slight suggestion of forward movement that would continue for three miles, leaving me little time to show everyone what I had trained to become. This time, I started near the front. Today's gun would mean run fast.

Once again, that was the plan.

Realistically, I knew the Bay to Breakers wouldn't be a victory lap to celebrate a new beginning but more of a final hurdle to greener pastures. One thing I know after four decades of waking up every day is that life is untidy. There's always an unresolved problem somewhere. But look! Just around the corner—no crowds, no clutter, no competitors. Victory over a life of semi-fulfilled goals, false starts, and scratching at the surface of things. I approached Sunday's race with this heavy cloud over my head, a resolve to inject more meaning into my life.

Can a race change you? I believe so. The original race organizers back in 1912 must have believed so, too. Conceived as a civic booster after the 1906 earthquake, the event was created to draw attention to San Francisco's rebirth from rubble and ash. The course, traversing from downtown (bay) to the beach (breakers), is also a path from devastation to renewal, from loss to gain, from destruction to new frontiers. It's poetic;

the ocean not a dead end but a clean slate. New life.

Sometime in the last one hundred years, though, the race became something else, co-opted by the champions of zaniness. Would this Bay to Breakers be a life-changing event for me or a Sunday jog with sixty thousand naked and drunk fools? Was I asking too much of a foot race? I slipped on the running outfit that went unused all week and set off to find out.

I went for a long warm-up on the Embarcadero. San Francisco's version of Mardi Gras was ahead, so I relished the last moments of calm as I ran at an easy pace along the waterfront. With thoughts of a speedy 12K, maybe a new personal record, I really felt like I was running back in time, back to that thirteen-year-old boy who anxiously stood on the starting line ready to prove to the world that he could run far and fast. Four blocks away people in costume started to appear. Weaving through the rear of the crowd lined up on Howard Street, I mingled with flamingos, Mr. Little Bo Peep, a guy in a diaper, and the infamous pink gorilla. Staying serious and focused was getting hard, especially when Jabba the Hutt lined up behind me for the Porta Potti. *This is a race, right?* Each corral behind mine was a block party, ready to go mobile at the sound of the starting gun. I strutted up to the seeded corral, milling about with faster guys. Quiet in our stretches and drills, we could hear the restless mass behind us.

Crack of the gun.

We were off, blazing down Howard Street at a 5:45-mile clip. The seeded group was a fast crowd. Running from the get-go felt like a goal accomplished in itself. *So this is what it feels like to run down Howard Street.* I felt fresh, thinking this might be my day.

And then he ran by me like I was running backward, Mr. Flawless Form in the new Nikes, blond dreads pulled back in a clip. The remainder of his running outfit was that there was no outfit. That did it. I couldn't hold back the laughter anymore. The paradox of a competitive runner competing in the buff was so funny, so absurd, so complete in its message that this race was not a stage for drama but rather for comedy, that I let go. It was liberating to finally let the laughter out. The baggage I had brought into this race was too heavy to run with, so I left it on the curb. *If we're not running to feel good, why are we running?* I carried this newfound lightness of heart and foot over Hayes Hill and into Golden Gate Park. Now relaxed, my pace quickened. Maybe I could catch him.

It would be poetic if I could write that my carefree attitude produced a new PR, but the reality is I was two minutes off. But I didn't care nor did I really spend much time gazing at the ocean looking for answers on the horizon. I felt complete, happy, maybe even joyful to let go of competition, the kind where I am trying to beat myself. What I really wanted to do was jog (did I say jog?) back up alongside the course to see the thousands of runners, joggers, walkers, revelers, and floats.

I could hear my grandmother's words again, "You're too hard on yourself." I started to get it. I was taking myself and my races much too seriously, only allowing myself one satisfactory outcome—a PR. Exactly who did I think I was?

The farther back in the pack, the happier everyone looked. No one wore the pained expression of pushing toward a goal pace or time. Today was about having fun. That's one thing humans do well, laugh and run. So why not put them together?

The Bay to Breakers is more celebration than race. I learned life doesn't always have to be a relentless drive forward. We can slow down and recognize who we've become, imagine who we might like to be, or celebrate the simple fact that we woke up that day to laugh easily at the years gone by. Some people call that living in the moment. A run is more than exercise. To be a runner is more than an identity. Running is more than proving you are fast.

Running is rebirth, every day.

I wanted to be reborn.

Feelings

After the predictable questions about my diet and sleep patterns, after various instruments gauged my bare body to measure its virility, and right about the time when I had had enough of the sterile, unsettling, fluorescent and Formica exam room, my doctor asked me a simple question that I found hard to answer.

"Why do you run?"

I rattled off the fitness benefits, the weight control, the challenges, but I started to bore even myself with my clichéd responses. She's a thoughtful woman, and she deserved a better response, so I stopped for a moment, reconsidered, and came up with

"It just feels good."

Runners get asked this question all the time because running looks silly to others. If we are truthful, we'll admit it's difficult to honestly answer the question of why we run. It's not that we don't have our reasons; it's that the desire doesn't stem from any immediate need. The urge is an enigma. Running at its most basic level is for pursuit or escape. Recreational sports re-create this fight or flight response. But running for running's sake, up and down the street? Why? Words don't communicate well my motivation to head out the door on a dark and cold morning. Saying I want to get in shape doesn't answer the question either since that doesn't explain why I choose running instead of swimming or tennis.

The two most common responses I hear in the general conversation among runners, especially about trail running, are

"to feel free" and

"to feel like a kid again."

They're kind of the same thing.

But the truth is that when I run, I don't actually free myself nor do I become a child again. I return to my commitments an hour or two later. I look in the mirror and see an adult. I just want to *feel* free. More simply, I just want to *feel*. When I run on trails, my experience is defined mostly by two senses, touch and smell. I don't really listen to anything because the steady rhythm of my footfall is my default focus. I don't crave the distraction of sounds. I want silence. Obviously, I'm not tasting anything. As for sight, though essential to the trail running experience, it is not necessarily why I am out there. I have had great runs through the monotony of the row houses of the Sunset District in San Francisco. If a vista opens up, I usually just stop and look, making sight the most effective of all distractions.

So that leaves touch and smell. That's why I am there.

That's why I run.

Scents from wild places arrive unannounced but always welcome. My sense of smell is strongly connected to my memory. A freshly fallen Douglas fir in July reminds me of Christmas. The smell of a eucalyptus tree brings to mind doing homework after school with my grandmother in Golden Gate Park. Scents are my photo albums, reminding me of the events that created who I am.

As for touch, on a trail run this sense is narrowed down to the soles of my feet meeting the earth. But that deliberate, mindful stepping on a dirt path through a forest stirs emotions in me, primitive feelings that feel true and real, if not confusing to my civilized mind. And it's all so different from the cultured pleasure I get by walking down a sidewalk. Touch is a reminder, too, of simple pleasures that can't be denied when encountered.

What a world of masquerades I find myself in—online maps, artificially flavored strawberry-kiwi iced tea, computer graphics in movies, lip-synched musical performances, scripted reality TV, virtual reality tennis. Nothing is real. So much artificiality that is sold as authenticity. It's easy to let entertainment, primarily of the visual variety, become the window to the world. But too much make-believe and falsehood, too much of always having the world interpreted for me, and I become a perpetual, passive tourist on a sightseeing bus, dabbling here and there as things pass through my frame of view. I know a little about a lot, but not a lot about anything.

If I am only entertained, never experiencing life myself,

then how can I know who I am? I can fool myself for a little while, but then I get stir crazy, my body restless, my mind craving something real to touch and experience. I can only read about other men's experiences in adventure magazines for so long. We were never designed to be stationary beings, using only our butts and eyes in passive activities. Feet were made for walking and hands were made for feeling. I have a need for authenticity, to discover those things that are so real and basic they need no explanation, such as a warm patch of sun, a blackberry, or the crashing of waves on sand. I want to feel. I want to be more than a member of the audience. I want my own life to be the show that entertains me. This is where running comes in.

    I remember the first time running helped me to craft a personal narrative that could make me proud. If I woke just a little earlier than usual, I could tack a run up Baker Beach onto my morning training for the Bay to Breakers. It was exhilarating at the six o'clock hour to feel like I owned that foggy western part of San Francisco, jogging down the middle of lonely Lake Street, the early morning hours quiet enough for me to hear the buzz of the high-pressure sodium street lamps. Baker Beach was mine for the taking, all mile and a half of damp sand and sea foam, all salt, musk, creepiness, and empty glory. I made the first tracks of the day, fancying myself a modern-day Robinson Crusoe. I felt so free from the obligation to be the team player that the middle of the day requires, so free from judgment, that one brave morning, I shed my shirt and shoes and ran nearly naked up the beach toward the

Golden Gate Bridge, nothing between me and my five senses but a pair of yellow nylon Sub4 running shorts. I didn't usually have that kind of nerve. I was more the shy, observant type, but no one was there to tell me if running almost nude was right or wrong. That's why it felt so good. I heard my voice and I listened. We are all sentient beings, making our choice to follow the rules or not. Running up the beach all alone, I felt like anything was possible. No one was there to tell me it wasn't. And for a boy who was suddenly growing up an only child away from his parents, that outlook felt necessary.

    I need to know, to feel with my own two feet, that beyond the artificial world I must live in, I still have the capacity to feel, that I'm not a robot, that I am still related to my caveman forbear, following in his deep footsteps on the right path, continuing his tenuous legacy of living his one and only life in epic desperation. Even though his concern for his physical survival has morphed into my concern for my sanity, it's all I've got. I want to run. But I do not need to in order to survive. When I go for a long trail run and it is tiring but not exhausting, hands on hips at the end, drawing deep breaths, I simply feel good about the effort, like I did something right. I am happy to be alive. Unlike my caveman forbear though, I have no physical reward from the effort in my bloody hands. It's just a feeling that my run was worth the effort. I hunted down authenticity.

    As my daily run got longer, I started to feel that the world was opening up to me, that I was pushing open a door someone tried to lock. Now, when I can't decide where to run,

I just visualize the valley I live in—the mountain to the south, the lakes to the west—and I create a route based on my past experiences, not an online map telling me where to go. And then I just go. The world becomes my treadmill. And instead of feeling guilty for all the ways in which we destroy the gift that is the earth, I start to see—no, to *feel*—one of the good things about being human: that I possess the endurance to get to where I need to go.

This was my answer to my doctor. This is why I run.

It was almost enough to convince myself.

Alexander Avenue Exit

"I wish I knew where I was going. I wish I could be more moderate in my desires, but I cannot, and so there is no rest."—John Muir

My daughter recognized the pattern.

"You like to wander off."

She had taken several of my stories about growing up and strung them together, discovering something I had failed to see.

I was three. My mother woke one morning to a phone call from the clerk at the Woodacre post office.

"Good morning, Pauline. Well . . . um . . . we have Alex down here."

This account is purely anecdotal as I was too young to remember, but as the story goes, I woke up early and left the house for a little morning exploration of our neighborhood. Good thing I had on my footie pajamas. My guess is that I simply wanted to check things out without the burden of having to hold a hand or follow instructions. Crack of dawn, everyone asleep, it was an opportunity I apparently took.

    I was seven. I was free to roam anywhere on our side of Crenshaw Boulevard in Torrance. The other side of Crenshaw? Nah-ah. My parents were liberal regarding my after-school activities as long as I followed the command to "stay out of trouble." On most days I had no reason to cross Crenshaw. It was a typical Southern California boulevard, six lanes of freeway-velocity traffic one didn't cross casually.

    But one day I was with a girl from the neighborhood who was my friend and no she wasn't my girlfriend, because I was too young for that, but somehow it was just her and me that afternoon. I don't recall her name, only that she was blond with blue eyes and lived a few houses down. As we spent that sunny afternoon walking the neighborhood, we roamed west to Crenshaw. I was so high off puppy love, I don't believe I even hesitated to push the crosswalk button. She was my partner in crime as we crossed Crenshaw and explored a new neighborhood replete with different playgrounds, houses of strangers, and greener grass. The thrill of getting somewhere new on our own superseded the threat of punishment for going somewhere we were told not to. In fact, west of Crenshaw was more alluring because it was off limits. I don't think this was the lesson I was supposed to learn.

But how did they find out, those only-there-when-you're-in-trouble parents of mine? How? My bliss was broken the moment I walked in the door and realized denial was not an option. My mother looked offended, as if to say, "How could you wander so far from your own neighborhood?" My stepfather, on the other hand, had the calm and eerily serene demeanor of a parent about to administer a serious ass whooping. I had disobeyed a direct order. There would be consequences. This is how it's done. Over bended knee, I struggled to breathe between each wallop. It hurt, but so what?

It was so worth it.

I was eleven. In San Francisco, ten-speeds were the transportation of choice not so much because they allowed us to travel farther but rather because we could get to places quicker. It didn't take long before I started to push the boundaries of distance again. I was now living with my grandparents, and they, too, gave me an ample amount of freedom after school. I was allowed, with a friend, to ride my bike across the Golden Gate Bridge. But only to the other side, where I was to then turn around at Vista Point and head back to the city. One day I saw the sign in the distance.

"Alexander Avenue."

It was like an invitation.

My friend was the smart one. He turned around. I couldn't, deciding right then and there at the northern end of the bridge that I was going to ride another two miles north into the waterfront town of Sausalito. It wasn't logical to me that the end of the bridge was the turnaround. I'd been to Sausalito once with my grandparents, so it wasn't completely unfamiliar. That day, though, I had a chance to be the new kid in town, to arrive on Main Street on my little steel horse, heads turning. "Who's he?" And for a boy who went from a broken home to his grandparents' care four hundred miles north in a new city, it was empowering to strike out on my own that afternoon. I learned that by the power of just my two legs, I could create a new reality for myself. I sat in a little park in downtown Sausalito eating a package of gummy bears while I watched tourists amble by, proud of the brave choice I had made but, truthfully, a little scared to be there by myself. I had reached the limits of my comfort zone, scared and excited all at the same time. Some guy asked me for change.

My grandmother found out about my adventure. How did she do it? How? My intercounty travels were suspended indefinitely, but hey, I had crossed the Golden Gate Bridge by myself, by my own accord, and under my own power.

Totally worth it.

I was 15. In Venice, Italy there are no streets and, so, no cars. My grandparents and I stayed at the Hotel Danieli just off the tourist track near the Campo San Maurizio, marked by a bell tower rising high above the four-story buildings. There is no rhyme or reason to Venice's layout. No blocks and grids, no concentric circles, no thoroughfares, few signs telling you which way to go. An overhead map of Venice looks like a regular city that has been compressed into a jigsaw puzzle pattern. The possibility for a visitor to get lost is high.

I was that visitor, and I wanted to get lost. That was my goal. From the time I came to live with them, my grandparents and I traveled extensively. To them, and to me now, travel means experiencing somewhere new. Very rarely did we visit the same place twice. Thanks to them, I am not too concerned with itineraries or maps. So with my grandparents' permission to explore Venice on my own one afternoon, I set out to do just that, leaving anything resembling a map behind. I started walking with no regard to direction, choosing the narrower *calle* when I had a choice. As I wandered away from the realm of tourists, I glimpsed Venetians living their daily lives: housekeepers hanging out laundry, elders pulling carts of groceries, bespectacled draftsmen working on drawings in cramped little offices. After an hour of navigating the corridors between centuries-old dwellings, I emerged onto a dirt square about the size of a basketball court. About twenty kids played a pickup game of soccer. One of them approached me, saying something in Italian, presumably an invitation to join the game. But having never played soccer or learned Italian, I smiled and shook my head no. He shrugged and jumped back into the match. Later, I would learn that part of Venice is called Ghetto Embraico.

When I started to see cars, I knew I had reached the outer boundaries of Venice. It was a good place to turn around, but I had the problem of not knowing exactly where to turn. Having twisted and turned my way into confusion, I had no idea how to get back to where I started. Deducing that continuing forward was the only way not to go, I did my best to navigate back toward the general direction of the hotel.

An hour of wandering finally brought me to a place where I could see the bell tower in the distance. Following a crooked path but always keeping the bell tower in sight, I thought I had it in the bag until, a mere quarter mile from my goal, I came upon the Grand Canal, somehow ending up on the opposite side of the waterway. If this had been the United States, I would have simply followed an expressway to the next overpass and easily found my way back. But this was Venice, and no such urban planning existed. I had to backtrack until I found passageways leading toward the setting sun, which I now used as a sort of westward beacon. Maybe I learned some of the ancient art of the Venetian *passeggiata* that afternoon, because I recall a budding deftness for getting from point A to point B, even if it meant sidetracking to points C, D, and E. I found the Ponte dell'Accademia easily, my gateway over the Grand Canal and back to the safety of the Hotel Danieli.

It's fair to say I spooked myself that day, thinking for more than a moment that I took too lightly the concept of getting lost in a foreign country. But with the necessity of finding my way with no help from either my grandparents or Italians whom I couldn't understand, I was keenly aware of my surroundings. I learned lessons I still carry around with me today—pay attention to where you are, take notes, remember.

I made it back six hours later. My grandparents said nothing, but when they lowered their shoulders, I could tell they were relieved. My timing was perfect as I learned, years later, that my grandmother was just moments away from calling the *Polizia*.

To this day I'm not good at sitting around. I could also tell you about the time in college I rode my moped around San Diego for three hours one night. Or of the times in Seattle, as a new resident, that I'd walk aimlessly around neighborhoods, exploring the city like a dog sniffing the perimeter. Or of the night I found myself six miles from my car running through a driving rainstorm on cliffside Conzelman Drive. The examples go on to the point where it becomes obvious I'm not a homebody. Each exploration rewarded me with a sense of adventure and the notion that there was more to the world than my backyard. I am not unique. I think all kids want to explore, but in my case I had no one holding me back.

I would call my wandering a bad habit that has produced good results. As lucky as I was to have trusting caregivers, I was just as lucky nothing bad happened to me. I am not boasting. I am aware that the ending to each of these stories could have been much worse. So it was almost comforting when my daughter announced her observation of me as a lifelong wanderer because seeing that pattern made me feel like there was a purpose to the movement. I was working on me, the nonnegotiable parts of my character that were trying to find an escape hatch. I told her once of my dream to own an old VW bus with a mini kitchen and camper, cruising up and down Highway 1.

"Yeah, but then we'd never see you." Appreciation for

my wanderlust was in her voice, but it was tinged with melancholy.

Where to, Pal?

I should be used to it by now. Before every marathon, I doubt myself, but the question the day before the 2009 New York City Marathon nagged like a splinter I couldn't pull out.

Why had I just traveled 2,500 miles to do what I could have done at home?

The short answer was that I had fuzzy memories of the 2006 NYC Marathon being exciting. A dozen marathons since that time made me doubt my memories, though. How much better could New York have been than Boston, San Francisco, Los Angeles, Seattle, or Portland? Better enough to be worth the effort to get there? Wherever I run it, it is still 26.2 miles.

My doubt turned to grumpiness at the expo when I got into the line to get into line. Though the number pickup was efficient, the crowd jostling for a sample here, a T-shirt there, was just too much for this laid-back Californian. Eat this, wear this, try this, buy this. The only thing I bought was a new headache and a new calf cramp. *Get me out of this place!*

I went from grumpy to cranky when I had to wake up at 3:30 a.m. to trek to the subway by 4:30 to catch the Staten Island Ferry by 5:30, all to be at the start area the required three *hours* before the 9:40 a.m. start. It was raining lightly upon my arrival but I came prepared with a Mylar sleeping sack. I retreated into my crinkly silver cocoon and did what I always do when I don't like how things are going. I went to sleep.

I awoke to a bizarre calm, a scene on mute, wondering for a moment if I had slept through the start. The rain had stopped, clouds lightened, and the climbing sun tried to pop through, forming a glowing gap of yellow in the overcast. Nearby, runners had settled into their own pockets of comfort, preserving energy for the work ahead, or that's what I assumed. Maybe we were all too focused on our own goals to confide to each other our worries, strangers too caught up in the idea of a perfect race to enjoy each other's company.

Wait, here's the likely reality—it's me. I do take myself too seriously. Why couldn't I just hang out with a few thousand like-minded souls, bonding over a shared nervousness? Why couldn't I drink that beer at the finish tent and loosen up? Why did I invest so much of myself into running? I appreciated the calm because I was in no mood for conversation. I was asking myself too many questions I couldn't answer, yet I couldn't turn it off.

As I stood in the starting corral, waiting to be herded onto the Verrazano-Narrows Bridge, I grew nauseated by the combined scent of peppery Icy Hot muscle rub and Porta Potti. When someone ate an overripe banana so close I could have peeled it for him, I felt like sitting down in defeat. *Let's get this thing started. I'm done with the marathon before the marathon.*

Then two things happened that changed everything.

A cannon fired, signaling the start of the marathon. Up on the bridge, close to the front of my wave, I turned to see the impressive sight of over forty-three thousand runners pressed up behind me.

Second, the cannon's boom triggered a roar from the crowd. Not the type of roar caused by a Super Bowl touchdown, but a deep, rolling cry released in unison.

In that moment, as the runners fore and aft, left and right, surged forward, I was no longer #6449 but rather part of a creature made up of 43,741 parts. We were as one, the 2009 New York City Marathon. That felt good because the only thing worse than suffering is suffering alone.

We locked into step almost immediately, not usual for such a large race. Through the early silence on the bridge, I could hear us breathing together like hundreds of black stallions. I felt no need to weave through the crowd because, for the first time that morning, I was happy to be one of the crowd.

No matter how many other marathons I had completed, nothing prepared me for the intensity of the crowds of New York that day, not even having run the New York City Marathon once before. No mere spectators, these two million cheering citizens were as much a part of the course support as the water stations and mile markers. In Brooklyn, men with Yankees caps and sausage fingers yelled "Brooklyn!" with so much authority and finality that I didn't need convincing that that was the place.

By the time we got to Queens, I realized I was hugging the right side of the road, collecting as much free energy from high fives as I could gather. Usually, I take in the crowd's energy in measured doses because I know the crowd support that helps me to drop my pace probably won't be there five miles down the road. But in New York I knew these people would be with me the entire distance, so I never left that curb. And I was right. I saw beautiful Manhattan women lose their prized cool. Their shouts were not of the "way to go" or "looking good" variety but more ecstatic yells of "Yeah!" and "Go!" Bronx kids stared at me with big doe eyes. I did my best to meet their gaze.

Cheers became frenzied screams as my part of the marathon mass sped through the final miles down Central Park. This was it, the big finale. My ears became a conduit for energy; their shouts of encouragement went right to my weary feet. On 59th Street, it was electric mayhem with the screams of a rock 'n' roll crowd and a guy with a bullhorn saying something about glory. I could have imagined it all, but it doesn't matter now, because I crossed the finish line a changed runner. I didn't feel like the same person who was so down on the race just three hours before, the person who questioned whether all the time and effort required to get to the starting line of the New York Marathon was worth it, the one who felt by himself on planet Earth.

I heard the answer to whether it was worth it loud and

clear in the passionate calls of the two million New Yorkers who lined the streets. They cheered our commitment, our strength, the sweat on our face, our willingness to suffer publicly, and our openness to the power of something done together instead of individually. New Yorkers knew that we, the marathon, were headed toward a place of transformation because New Yorkers had got to where we were going a long time before.

Life is hard in New York. Struggle is nothing new. It's all black or white. It's all life or death. The cars drive fast, the wind is cold, and the streets are rough. It's not necessarily a bad thing, especially if you believe easy is not always better. I am from the California coast though, where this concept can be hard to find along the sunny beaches. The coast is clean and simple, but life is not that way. New York's air is seamy and earthy, like the breath we exhale. If California is what we dream, then New York is what we wake up to. New Yorkers struggle together daily, all eight million of them. And their triumphs are sweeter because they share the hardship side by side, just like a marathon. We don't have to suffer alone. There are helping hands when we are down. When I turned my gaze away from myself, I saw those hands. And yes, I know marathons are trite when compared to living in poverty or fearing for your life, but it was still hardship. That ought to carry some merit.

All this communion from a cloudy November morning, 2,500 miles from home and 26.2 miles from the runner I used to be. I was on my way to a different me.

Off the Bench

"They need a coach." You know the movie.

"We heard the other schools have a cross-country team and we were thinking . . ."

My life was neatly organized to eliminate surprises. Then this dilemma fell into my lap. "Me, coaching material?" The role seemed so opposite of my personality. I fly low, preferring to be below the radar, just off the center of attention. While people in my small town know me as "the runner," it's a title I try to shrug off. There are a lot of runners here.

With this implied request, I had to confront the progress of my character and ask what kind of adult I had become. I hemmed and hawed, tirelessly deliberating in my overly analytical, messed-up mind. In the end I felt compelled—no, obligated—to take the job.

"We know how much you love running so we thought . . ."

Did I have a choice?

This movie should be called *Whirlpool*.

I had been talking up cross-country to my ten-year-old daughter since we started running 5Ks together, saying, "Just wait until you get to middle school and high school when you can run on a cross-country team! You know how fun that'll be?" I could tell she was interested but sensed her hesitation to be part of a team, intimidated to have others rely on her ability to perform. So here was a test of my worth as a father in the eyes of my daughter. I had the opportunity to start the cross-country team I was raving about.

Kids recognize when you are genuine, and this was my time to show her I meant what I said.

I was really nervous before the first practice. Though I had been a teacher and a summer camp counselor, some time had passed since I'd worked with kids, and I had never taught children how to run. But my anxiety dissipated almost immediately when I sent them out on their first warm-up lap. They were like horses running free. In a beautifully natural way, they wanted to run.

Though I had many games planned throughout the season, when it came down to it they just wanted to move. I could see the strength they gained by running as a group on the field, down the little bit of single track on the edge of campus and around school buildings (after years of being told "Walk!"). For these kids, this was a new and exciting way to run, and it gave them confidence in their own ability. Keeping up always feels good. While they ran they laughed, egging each other on and staggering in with melodramatic exhaustion. They imagined themselves a native tribe, roving over terrain in search of game or enemy factions. Kids love pretending, trying on the hats of their foes and emulating their heroes.

I passed out jerseys at the next practice. Their eyes lit up. Suddenly we were a team and it was official.

"Can we keep these?"

"Yes."

"Cool!"

I don't get a chance to spectate at races very often. There's always talk of how uplifting watching a marathon is, but when I hear, "You're awesome, go runner!" from some stranger, all I think is, *Uh, Ok. I'm just plugging along*. But after seeing my team participate in their first cross-country meet, I knew that to witness people being passionate, pushing themselves through pain, enduring—that is inspiring.

But as any runner knows, it is not always fun and games. Sometimes the price of competition is disappointment. At the second meet, two of the fourth grade runners in the lead pack took a wrong turn, veering too far off course to stay in contention. They returned to the finish area all tears. I had wanted cross-country only to be about blue skies—those days when everything feels so easy and goes your way. I mistakenly assumed that youthful determination would be enough to bring all of my runners to that place, but I was wrong. Sometimes, even when you have done all you can, life tries to extinguish your flame. So I was caught unprepared, not knowing exactly how to deal with their disappointment. I didn't even know what to say to those runners who came in last, let alone the ones that ran off the course. I wanted to offer up wisdom to keep their little fires burning, but I came up with nothing. What could I say? Every line I came up with sounded like a platitude. *"You'll get them next time," "I am glad you tried your best."* It was a terrible thing; no way around it. The best I could do for damage control, I figured, was not make it worse. So I kept quiet, but that didn't feel right.

    The verbal aspect of being a leader is difficult for me. After that day, I became very conscious of how I spoke to the kids as a coach. Keep it honest, I reminded myself, because they'll see through false accolades. But I'd still catch myself saying things like, "Get up there!" and I wouldn't like the sound of my voice. At their age it is not so much about placing first but rather about trying their best. When I yelled those coach-like phrases I thought were expected of me, I felt like I was pretending to be someone I wasn't. I'd rather inspire my runners in quieter ways, with a nod that shows I believe in them or little "Good running" whispers after a relay at practice. Now uncovered was my real motivation to coach this team—to give these kids the coach I rarely had. I knew what I wanted to be, just not how to become it. This is where my own history got in the way.

    I had a string of bad coaches, starting with my first one. He was the coach of the first basketball team I played for when I was eight. "Played" might be an overstatement as I probably had less than ten minutes court time the entire season. Admittedly I wasn't very good. But there was no effort by the coach to make me feel as if I was part of the team regardless of my lack of talent. Every game, this coach, this now-faceless figure in my memory, would put me in for the last two minutes of the first quarter, probably to appease my folks. The break in periods was a convenient and distracting time to pull me back out. I recognized this routine and watched the last three quarters from the bench, fully aware of how inconsequential I was to the game's outcome. I wore the uniform, but I felt like an outsider.

    I was skeptical about team sports for several years after my basketball experience. But reasoning that I had some experience in distance running, having run the Bay to Breakers, I decided to run track as a high school sophomore. I tried out for the distance team. But after a week of watching the talented front-runners quickly pull away, I felt frustrated that what little ability I had was not enough to keep up. But I did know that hard work was a big factor in distance running, and I was willing to pay my sweat equity. My guess was that eventually all of this heavy breathing would amount to something. That was until the distance coach coasted up next to me on his bike during one of my lag-behind runs and casually said, "You know, Alex, it's just not gonna happen."

    To this day I don't know whether he wanted to test my mettle or if he was being brutally honest to spare me the embarrassment. Unfortunately, I'll never know because that was the extent of the comment. There was no "But if you work at it . . ." Nothing, no follow through. My legs felt instantly listless. What's the point? I was so discouraged, I gave up.

But to my advantage, they did not cut kids who wanted to run track, so I jumped to the sprinting squad. Still not very good but with renewed resolve, I showed up to every practice with a willingness to train hard. I wanted to be a good runner even if I didn't know what the heck I was doing. During interval sessions, the coach would yell and prod the faster kids from the infield when they walked between reps instead of jogging. While I was doing everything I could to stay on my feet and keep my breakfast down, there was a pregnant pause when I walked by him. I worked hard but didn't improve. How could I with no guidance? I just needed a little direction, someone to grab my shoulders from behind and say, "This way." All I wanted was a shot to prove myself, to reinvent myself as a young man who was ready to work for something. I had hoped running was my ticket as it had been before.

All the nausea in my head and searing pain in my lungs, the burning in my quads and soreness in my hip flexors, it must be making me a better runner, right? Silence from the coach. He tolerated me, at best. *Do I embarrass you? Would an ounce of encouragement kill you?* A coach's detachment is his tacit dismissal of you. He's given up on you. Most meets, I was tossed into the second heats, those races for the extra kids that don't count for points. Was I feeling sorry for myself? Maybe a bit, but why go through the pretense of coaching a team without doing your best to try to make all members feel essential? Was it just about winning? Years later when I mentioned to my high school track friend that I thought the coaches really only coached the top guys he said, "You didn't know that?" I guess the joke was on me, the outsider. And I'd thought I was on the team.

As an adult competitor, I train hard with occasional good results. A large part of my motivation to do well is just to spite my old coaches. *Look, see? I told you I could be good.* And when I win races or my age group, I mentally thumb my nose at them. But I know that kind of motivation is for all the wrong reasons. That ship sailed twenty-five years ago. As an adult I'm rarely a team player, tending toward the individual endeavor instead of the group experience. Now I know where I got it from. Coaches ought to be aware of the power of their comments, the ability of eight words to kill a kid's passion. Maybe this is why I fell silent trying to console my wayward runners. I was scared of the damage I might do. Looking back now, I wonder what my silence said.

There is a hero in this history, a Mickey to my Rocky. The coach of the neighborhood little league team was an overweight pipe fitter named Frank. I don't think he knew a lot about baseball, but he seemed to get a kick out of us kids. To make a gross generalization, there are two types of fathers, those that want their sons to be what they themselves were not and those, like Frank, who love their kids for who they are. Frank smiled a lot and knew everyone's name right off the bat. He offered an extra day of batting practice for the kids that just liked to whack the ball as far as they could. He was our after-school father, protecting our dreams of hitting in the winning run.

Since the only requirement to be on the team was that

you had to be born between x and y date, there was a wide range of talent. Baseball was a sport I was good at, so I enjoyed the games. But no matter how big a lead we had, at the top of the fourth in every game, Coach would take out the best players and put in the ones still learning their chops.

"Why?" we'd screech.

"Because they are on the team too." He let us know these kids weren't just strangers taking up space in the dugout but players, people who had the same desire to win as we hotshots did. Coach showed us that what you do, as much as what you say, makes others feel included. He emphasized that we were a team above everything else, including winning. The funny thing is, though, I remember doing lots of winning. Sometimes the lesser talented of us would rise to the occasion, catching a fly ball or getting a hit. The rest of us loved it, gaining a newfound respect for these teammates. His lasting lesson was that the value of team sports is the strength we get from inspiring one another. The winning follows.

My grandfather and I once spotted Carlos Santana in a restaurant sitting nearby. All through my meal, I tried to come up with something witty to say to one of my rock and roll heroes, something that showed my true appreciation. But my grandfather, never one to overthink things and always one to act on impulse, just pointed to him as we passed and said matter-of-factly, "You're great."

Carlos's face lit up. "Just a reflection of your light, sir," he said, as if to say, *"I'm only as good as you believe me to be."*

Carlos Santana would make a good coach too.

Thirty years later, one of my cross-country runners said to the other runners out of the blue, "We run better as a team."

This is the beauty of cross-country, and it's the simple and quiet truth I had been looking for, buried and forgotten in my past. While running may be an inherently selfish activity, if we make it a team sport, then everyone, regardless of ability, has a part to play. We all have worth. We all belong.

Our community is small. I'll see my cross-country runners grow to be teenagers. Some will look the other way when they are up to no good. Some may smile and wave. Either way I hope they think, *Hey, that's my cross-country coach. That was fun.* That'll be my future payoff—these little runners remembering years from now, when they are moody, withdrawn teens or shy volunteer coaches, that they weren't alone. They knew they were an essential part of the team. They caught my reflection. Then, with the cameras still rolling, I will have finally played my part.

Moment of Silence

One morning my ten-year-old daughter asked if she could walk to school on her own. We had a routine of walking together every morning, so I asked her half-jokingly, "What, you don't want to walk with *me*?"

"I just want to walk by myself today," she said in all seriousness.

I gave her permission and let her go because what she was really asking for was a moment of silence. Her life is filled with a medley of noise without an apparent theme. As a parent I either chuck directives at her—"get ready for school," "clean your room," "go to bed"—or occupy her free time with material I think is worth her attention, like that bad eighties song she still doesn't like. But for myself, I know that I need a break daily, time and space to think, to ponder everything or nothing.

I have no idea what went through my daughter's head on her way to school that morning. Maybe she practiced spelling words for a test or avoided cracks in the sidewalk. It didn't matter; it was none of my business. I gave her the quiet morning to walk. If I had bombarded her with questions about it later, I would have taken the morning right back.

When I was her age, I had an easy nine-block stroll to school. I always walked alone. The time belonged to me, not parents or teachers, and not having to talk for twenty minutes was a relief that allowed me to wonder about the past (*What did Elizabeth mean by that?*), the present (*Cool car!*) and the future (*What's down that alley?*). But I had to take it a step further when, in eighth grade, I was confronted by a friend who became a bully to me. He was successful at making my life miserable, turning other kids against me, and shaking my self-confidence by punctuating everything I said with a dismissive "tsst." I couldn't sleep. I couldn't eat. I lost fifteen pounds.

When I woke in the predawn hours with a knot in my stomach, I knew laying in bed wasn't going to make my situation any better. I packed my lunch into my backpack, grabbed my basketball, and headed to Rochambeau Playground near school at 6:30. I had a quiet solid hour to shoot hoops by myself before Tai Chi practitioners and the first kids started to arrive. My red, white, and blue basketball made a ping slap noise on the asphalt that echoed purely, not tainted by the "tsst" that made my skin crawl. San Francisco fog sat gently on my scene, cozy and private. I shot from every conceivable angle. I experimented with different techniques without concern of looking foolish. I began to plot my defense.

I needed this quiet hour to figure out what to do. I needed silence for myself to carry on. I can be a loner. Sometimes it is hard for people around me to understand that I don't want their voices in my head. By waking early and getting to that playground before everyone else, I felt in control. It was empowering. Nobody else did it. With the quiet to think, I saw with swish after swish that I was, in fact, good at something. Someone could have told me that, but during those hard months, I wouldn't have believed them. I needed the tangible proof you can only gather yourself. My confidence returned. I became the captain of the basketball team. And the bully got his one day when, tired of yet another episode, I took that same basketball I practiced with every morning, shoved it into his chest to pin him against the wall, looked him square in the eye, and simply said, "Stop." He did. My solution required silence to be recognized for its simplicity.

I run daily because running gives me the silence to problem solve away from the problem itself. Sometimes the problem is just static and distortion, and the run in and of itself is all I need. There's a trail that I return to, usually after a busy day, that is the most quiet path I have found around the lakes near my home. It travels along the forested shoreline, padded by conifer needles that dampen my footfalls. I always stop at the same bend under a fir, let the sweat dry, and wait for my breathing to return to normal. Then I just stand there and take in the silence. I think about everything that is probably happening in the world, and I am relieved that, for the time being, I'm not part of it. The silence swallows everything. The quiet moment is precious.

When I continue my run, the silence is so powerful that it has seeped into my subconsciousness. The sound of my steps is erased, and I stride in a Zen-like state. Then, with my mind's slate wiped clean, ideas start to trickle in, seemingly from thin air. My brain needs the same break that my muscles do. When I run I can disengage from work, obligations, even time. My mind gets to run free. And it takes me to some fitting solutions and wild places. The solutions arrive like the sunrise, unannounced and undeniable. My daughter was waiting for it to get light.

For those that are young and on their way to school, moments of silence are there waiting, once Dad learns to be quiet.

Art versus Science

Now or later? That's the question I increasingly asked myself as I became a more serious runner, struggling with the daily run versus the twice yearly race. The best runs I remember were impulsive, like I was a whimsical artist at work when I branched off on a new trail or picked up the pace for no other reason than it felt good in the moment. On the other hand, the best races I've had came after the diligent following of a training plan, each run prescribed at a set pace and distance weeks ahead of time, all in the name of getting me to the start line in the best possible shape. There was no spontaneity. It was sometimes dull and always predictable running, but it provided the best results. Training was a scientific experiment. In my experience, neither approach leads to balance or fulfillment. Do I focus my running on doing well in two marathons a year, skipping, say, a long run in Point Reyes with friends on a clear morning because I'm tapering for a marathon four days later with a chance for a PR? Or do I accept mediocre race performances in exchange for an approach that lets whim take me where it will?

Art versus Science. Here is how I imagine the extremes of both:

If I were the scientist, I'd rise every day at 6:10 to head out for my four-mile trot on the paved bike path around the lake in the park. Returning at 6:45, I'd start the coffee and oatmeal and clean up for my 9-to-5. There would be a latte everyday at 10:00 a.m. whether I really want it or not because it's just what I've always done. Afternoons would drag. I'd cross days off on the calendar.

That evening I would ponder all the things I was interested in trying, but each idea would always be punctuated by a logical excuse. I could swim at the local pool in the morning, but it'd be too cold. I could volunteer for little league coaching, but the kids wouldn't listen to me. I could take that weekend trip down the coast, but it would probably rain. I wouldn't be good with changes in plans. My practicality would keep me safe from harm, treading the tepid and shallow waters of a ho-hum life. At best, I'd be a surface scratcher. But I'd make deposits into my savings account, go to the dentist every six months, and change the oil every three thousand miles.

And my running? After several years of the same old loop at the same old pace, my body's fitness would plateau without a different stimulus to become stronger, though I would be injury-free. My body would be primed for a PR performance, but the motivator wouldn't be there, so those performances would be frustrating in their inconsistency, arriving in small increments. Numbers would become boring, but without meaning ascribed to my running, it's all I'd have. My running life would lack the mystery and adventure that gives it passion. I would be fast, but all I'd be to an outside observer would be a bib number.

But the appeal in this approach would be persevering through the grind and setting a personal best on marathon day. I haven't always been a process kind of person. Sometimes I like results, something tangible to look at to feel proud of myself. But what happens when the numbers are no longer enough to fulfill me, when the athleticism just feels like exercise?

One of the games that I play with the cross-country team I coach is the donut relay, a twenty-two-lap race. They take turns running a lap, while I run every lap. It's the team versus me. If they beat me, which they have done three out of three times, I buy donuts for them. They run with fervor and cheer each other on, unlike in any other activity I ask them to do. I motivate them. I'm a good coach.

Or am I? Are they reveling in the joy of competition and the satisfaction of running their absolute best? Or are they simply answering the siren call of sugar? I might have won every time if the prize had been more healthy.

I began to question the merits of the donut relay when a parent of one of the runners expressed her dissatisfaction with the offering of food as a reward, especially junk food, for running. At first I defended the race as a way to show kids how much they can do when they are really motivated. I wanted them to see what I saw when they tried their best. An earnest child is a beautiful thing, pushing and clawing for life to give them more. If it took a donut to bring that forth, so be it.

She countered, "Food should be for nourishment and for socializing, not for rewards. I know adults who "reward" themselves with desserts or fat-laden foods and they're usually overweight, with eating patterns that started in childhood. Once junk food is introduced, that's what kids expect." After some thinking, I've come to believe she is right.

I'd like running to be its own reward. When did its benefits—fitness, health, friendly competition—become insufficient? On hot practice days, kids look at me like "Where's my popsicle, mister?" After the races I run, my friends and I pick up our event T-shirts while a finisher medal dangles around our neck. We're spoiled children who expect a reward. It starts to feel silly and meaningless and unnecessary that we need something that has nothing to do with running to tell us we did a good job running.

We doubt ourselves and then let our ego take over, giving in to an urge to let everyone know how noble we think we are because we chose a difficult sport. Did I run for the glory or for the donut? I'm guilty too, having enjoyed the back-patting from others. And I wear that New York City Marathon shirt all the time. It starts with a donut and ends with you bragging about 26.2 on a bumper sticker while you listen for someone to say, "That's pretty good." I was listening too while I ran for treats. I think for most talented runners, their athleticism is enough. Their numbers evoke a deep pride. They know they are elite, different, the best of the best. The science of it all is encouraging. I am a good runner, but I am not talented. My ability does not allow me to dream of the Olympics. For me, science alone is not enough. The numbers ran out of appeal.

If I were the Artist, I would find a clean room in a shared rental and eat every meal over brown rice. I'd find a job, anything, that paid just enough money to cover my expenses but no more. This setup would allow me ample time to run every day, lacing up around 3:00 p.m. and running until the sun set, fifteen miles daily.

Come weekends I'd strap on my hydration pack, stash a few energy bars in the pockets, and get lost all day crossing bridges, traversing ridges, exploring the lengths of boulevards, running through neighborhoods I'd only driven through, headlamp stowed in case I was out until dark.

Upon my return home, I'd stretch my hamstrings, eat a big piece of salmon cooked just right, write until I started nodding off and be asleep by nine. Races would be peppered into the schedule every two weeks, new-to-me courses in unfamiliar terrain, and three to four marathons raced yearly. Prepared by weeks of big miles, I'd do well enough but not great.

Day in and day out, year after year, on my solo quest to spend as much time on my feet as possible, I'd be dedicated to the religion of running, like a monk in the mountains, like a painter in his studio running through canvases like scratch paper until,

    . . . two years into it, I'd be crumpled on the living room floor nursing this or that injury, desperately trying the latest stretch, wondering what happened, anxious and burnt out and trying to decide if I even liked running anymore. What did I have to show for all of the running except for worn-out shoes? The process was good, but where was it leading me? And if this were the artistic approach, what would I be trying to express? What am I trying to say?

    I'd have no one to turn to, having ignored every relationship for the sake of the run.

    I'd have nothing else to do, having adopted "runner" as my sole identity.

    I would be lost, dedication turned into obsession.

    Which way should I go?

    It's the *how* that can be as hard to find as the *what*. Knowing I am not the first to walk down these roads and ancient paths, sometimes I still just want some gentle hands to turn my shoulders from behind and whisper, "This way." It would be a little rest for my soul.

    I suspect there is a third approach to running—or sailing or knitting or oil painting or whatever is one's passion—that could give me that perfect balance that I seek but rarely find. How about a willingness to follow my passions not with reservation but with deliberation to find meaning in the chaos? Earnestly seeking answers while accepting I may never find them, letting experiences compliment and build upon one another to take me to places I couldn't have imagined a year earlier, training toward a vision, building some art, crafting my message, like an inventor who loves to tinker, a filmmaker who enjoys the dailies, a writer who knows the plot but not how to get there yet.

Fittingly, I call this third approach literature. I don't run just to run, because it's a blessing and a curse that I have to look for meaning in everything I do. I am an artist, specifically a writer, looking for my story, run after run, race after race, draft after draft. As I run, I record my thoughts in my head. When I am fastidious, I write them down. Half of my story is written in miles completed. The other half I am writing every time I step out the door. I want to know why I do the things I do. And I want to know the plot.

"I can win, I can win, I can win." —***Billy Mills, runner and scientist***

"Believe, believe, believe." —***Billy Mills, runner and artist***

The Billy Mills story is simple, a victory that came from behind on the last lap of the 1964 10,000M Olympic final in Tokyo. During his training, Mills said he visualized winning. Though he was boxed in on the last lap, he clung to his vision and proceeded to carry out the kind of race he believed he was capable of running. I like to put myself in his head, imagining running past the world's best like they were statues. I'd like to run a mile in his shoes, knowing I was capable of doing something great and having the opportunity to do it.

I did have a Billy Mills moment a few Sundays ago, albeit on the streets of San Francisco instead of an Olympic stadium. I wasn't going for a win but rather a sub-thirty-nine-minute 10K. The similarity was found in the approach to our races. Prior to my own 10K, I had some good training under my belt. Workouts felt easy and produced the kind of fast times that would allow me to reach my goal pace. Standing on the start line, I had the confidence that I could bring forth what I knew to be true, that I could run six miles at the pace I had set for myself. That was the vision I had crafted with hard work. My experiences up to that point told me it was true. I allude to Billy Mills because he mastered both artistry and science, his training gave him the truths with which to paint his future. A scientist believes in facts. An artist believes in vision.

I ran 38:54. A solid and consistent race, though nothing as flashy as Billy Mills's finish. Was it hard? Yes.

Unlike sports that don't involve a racing component, to run better (faster) involves pain. Basketball, football, and baseball are reactive sports. To play them better doesn't require that you throw the ball harder but rather that you make good decisions and throw the ball more accurately. In running, if I want to beat the guy in front of me or set a new personal record, that task involves pain and discomfort. While jogging is easy and running is comfortably hard, racing hurts. On a regular basis, I put myself in a position to hurt. But I'm not complaining. I know this is part of the deal. I actually like it.

Those of us who take running to heart accept pain, for it's our marker that we are doing all we can do with our toil and effort. What gets me through my time in the pain cave is the faith in my ability that was shaped through the hard work of training. Experience teaches me what is possible while allowing me to be patient in the suffering. During a marathon, especially in the final miles when I am really pushing and clinging to hope, faith draws me through the difficulty with the promise of reaching a level of performance I've neared but haven't yet had the opportunity to touch. It's a level I believe to be attainable, if only because I felt its edges during training, dipping down to a low pace, running a few extra miles on empty, successfully venturing out of my comfort zone. This sounds pompous to me, but my faith in myself is not as a 2:14 marathoner but as a runner who can redline for a full twenty-six miles. That's my experience. In the throws of striving for something higher, there is no good reason to give up unless I don't believe in myself. I admire the way Billy Mills turned talent into faith.

I like the idea of faith, but I want to work for it and earn it because I don't think faith can be handed over like a baton. I want to believe in myself, but I want to get to that belief through earned experience, punching my ticket with each first step of every run. My suspicion is that the best path toward faith, as in running, is not in fits and spasms but in a quiet and even-keel search for answers in the little occurrences of everyday life. The way I've built a faith in my running could be the way to build a belief in something beyond myself—working hard to stack experiences into something meaningful. I want all of this running to add up to something. When there is evidence before me, I want to have the capacity and courage to believe what I see. As the writers I appreciate create stories that are believable, I too want to write a story filled with the truths I've found.

It would be a stretch to call myself religious, but, as a runner, I wonder if I share the same daily habits as those practicing their own faiths. I take running seriously. I run daily, avoid junk food, strengthen my core, do all those little things I've learned are important, read about running, write about running, coach running, and generally let it seep into most aspects of my life. I believe that smart and diligent training can make me better in the same way that those who are religious follow the tenets of their faith to reach a conviction beyond the rituals themselves. Daily I build the belief in my ability that gives me strength both physically and mentally to go for it. Running showed me faith is possible.

But if I am taking the literature approach, what is my message?

When I see runners at races, I see billboards:
"I'm recovering."
"I'm losing weight."
"I'm running from the past."
"I'm strong."
"I am moving forward."

We all have something to say, in the expediency of our stride, in the grimace on our face, in the color of our singlet. I've trained as hard as I could. I've run as fast as I could. I actually got the faith I was looking for, yet something feels unanswered, something is not being heard, like I am yelling and nothing is coming out, as if I am asking a question instead of carrying a message. Maybe this is my motivation, waiting for a voice I can believe to say, "That's pretty good." So while I may preach the model of inner strength and motivation to the kids I coach, I simultaneously struggle to be that runner myself. I am calling out, and waiting for an answer.

I needed a call back to keep going, to make it to some end and feel it was all worth it. What was the point of all this faith? Was there a running heaven? I needed more from my story because just faith in my running wasn't enough. I wanted to find the answer to why I was running so hard just to believe in myself.

Dearest Alex

April 26, 1987

Dearest Alex,

A retreat to me means reflections of things past, present and times yet to be. So I guess I have set the theme for this letter.

It must have started from the time you asked us for "Coco-Lola" or "Coco-Lolo." We've enjoyed your companionship and presence. Academically, you have proven yourself worthy of your grades. Bravo! Personally, you have grown well and handled your relationships with great care.

The present seems to be heading well. You have maintained a great gift, direction. If you only knew how many young adults don't have that knack.

Now, about the future and your

anticipations. Don't be afraid to dare, to challenge, and seek answers. The alternative is dismal. Your greatest gift to us would be knowing that you are there, looking, testing, working hard for your beliefs.

There are only two areas that worry me (after years of Alex-watching!). First, you are a little too hard on yourself sometimes. Ease up—it is vital for survival. Second, your well-known stubbornness. Try to be more flexible to avoid stress—the big killer of males, ok?

We have been through, and seen a lot, the three of us, a chain I hope we won't ever break.

Big guys cry, and pray, so don't be afraid to do either. But most of all be kind to yourself, accept your shortcomings when they exist.

You have earned my love, trust and respect. I am counting on a continuance of those feelings. Joe and I will always be here for you. He and I agreed that our commitment to you would be total, from the day you first came to us—count on it.

With much love,
Lola

Keep On Keepin' On

In 1978, when I was still new to the Bay Area, the Portofino Apartments in Sausalito caught my attention one night on a drive home to San Francisco with my grandparents. Tucked into a steep shoreline, they overlook a small but picturesque cove less than a mile from the Golden Gate Bridge. Harbor lights twinkle below on the surface of the water. In the way that the multistoried buildings used every bit of land to claim their spot on the hillside, they had a Richard Scarry–village feel that I found very appealing. I liked hidden, interlocking, and quirky. Like most kids, when my world was expanding, I wanted miniature and close at hand. It also helped that there was a black 1973 Porsche 911S parked in the rooftop carport, which I figured came with the place. I believed that someday I would drive that Porsche. It was just a matter of time. I also assumed I'd be alone and that someday this would be the pad where I'd live until I figured out how I wanted to conduct my middle years.

Someday is here, and I drive a 1992 Toyota pickup. I am in those middle years now. Never moved into those apartments, can't afford the sports car. Other dreams and ideas pushed that one aside. Looking back, it was easy to forget.

Which is not to say I am disappointed but to say that things didn't turn out quite like I wanted them to. When do they? I see that black Porsche from the seventies now, and I'm that kid that believes anything is possible—baseball player, astronaut, gold medalist. Adulthood takes that outlook away for all but a select few of us. For a long time I didn't worry so much about not having a Porsche, because the guys driving them were always older. I still had time. Now they're my age or, worse, younger.

But when I find myself on the boardwalk across the water from the Portofino at night, I can still recognize that part of me that would like to smell the ocean every morning, to hear the sound of little waves splashing against seaside rocks, to sometimes hear a fog horn in the night.

I don't know what happened to all of those years in between. At some point in adulthood, it became easier to cross dreams off my list than to add them to it. One of the best years of my life was 1987, when I graduated from high school and then, three months later, packed up and drove six hundred miles by myself to start college. Those were some ground swell changes I had little difficulty accepting. I remember feeling nervous but not scared, past the point of making excuses to find a way out. I also remember feeling anything was possible.

As I got older, I got good at distracting myself, piles of

guidebooks and magazines stacked neatly on the coffee table. Distractions became the new dreams, anything to avoid asking, "What do I really want?" What's more, I got used to sitting around and waiting for the answer to come to me like a million-dollar check in the mail instead of getting up and seeking the answer through the trials and errors of life.

I think one of the hardest things is to have something so close you can smell it and feel it and you want it and all you have to do is reach out and grab it, but you've told yourself for so long that you can't do it, and then it slips away. The words of doubt and disbelief from others that you would have righteously rebelled against as an earnest young adult you now accept as truth, while your own wistful dreams and ideas you choose to forget. One of my fears in life is of moments slipping away, of opportunities lost. It is sad when we are content to let dreams stay dreams, even sadder when dreams become footnotes, and saddest when dreams go back to fantasy. Dreams are unfinished business.

I know it's a shallow gauge, but to me the Porsche represented dreams. Call me vain but from an early age I wanted to be well known. Maybe I spent too many hours listening to vinyl by myself in the basement, admiring the rock star in the mirror with a brush for a microphone. Not Abraham Lincoln famous, more Henry David Thoreau famous, appreciated later, fame finding me like an album or book pulled from dusty stacks. People would know my name, and they'd associate it with intrigue. Sometimes this desire to be recognized feels more like a fantasy.

Where did I get this belief in my own potential, or in more accurate terms, how did I get so arrogant? I attribute a lot of it to my high school, Saint Ignatius College Preparatory. I graduated with the confidence that I could choose not just my own path in life, but that I could choose any path. SI, as we called it, was very good at highlighting each of our strengths. They were even better at telling us that God didn't give us these talents, nor were they spending all their time educating us so that we could simply improve our own standing in the world by, say, getting rich and buying a Porsche. On the top of every assignment we were required to write "AMDG"—*Ad majorem Dei gloriam.* For the greater glory of God. Knowledge and wisdom were not to be hoarded selfishly. Our talents and gifts were to be used for the service of others. In fact, that was the SI creed—"In the service of others." Our job was to figure out how we were going to do that. My English teacher, Mr. Jim Bjorkquist, wrote on the bottom of one of my better essays, "Alex, a lot has been given to you and so a lot will be asked." These are words I've struggled with since then. What is being asked?

After graduation we had a confidence that out in the world we had a calling, something we'd be good at and were meant to do. All SI asked for was a belief in ourselves and a promise that we wouldn't settle for the easy path, the one that asks nothing. We would search for truth and meaning, sifting through the parts of our lives like they were a pile of jigsaw puzzle pieces. The solution was there, but the puzzle wouldn't put itself together. We'd find pieces that fit together into a bigger picture that answered the question "What do I do?"

That approach is easier said than done. Twenty-four years later, I've earned a film degree, taught at an elementary school, and now work as a carpenter. Decent and honest professions, but not necessarily my callings. The weighty edict SI laid on us has made finding a career that is meaningful to me a challenge. I promised not to settle.

Four times a year I open my mailbox to find *Genesis*, the alumni publication of SI. No black and white newsletter, *Genesis* is a full-color magazine printed on heavy stock and filled with the accomplishments of 156 years of graduates—governors, Hall of Famers, diplomats, screenwriters. To flip through the magazine is a humbling experience, and I put it down feeling a bit incompetent, wondering exactly what I have accomplished. You don't get a six figure salary or a wall plaque for sticking with it. It's no fun being called out on a quarterly basis.

The latest issue of *Genesis* was about digging deeper and finding the meaning in life around us. From former SI president Father Walsh at a commencement ceremony:

"Ponder the ancient and lasting philosophical and theological questions and avoid shallow answers . . . wisdom and understanding take work, are laborious, and demand your undivided attention."

It's a very good theory but a hard practice. A quarter century later, I'm still wondering what my gifts are as I watch my peers excel. I haven't given up. I'm still looking, and I won't settle. But damn, it's hard at times to feel what you do is meaningful to yourself. What's easy is doubt. Maybe the path will become clearer, if not easier, when I find the answer to that burning question that will not go away—what am I being asked?

There are two things I really like to do—running and writing. I don't know if I am that good at either, but I've never had to be asked twice to do them. However, I've never taken these pursuits seriously beyond something I do when I am not working. But looking closely at my off time I see that these two activities are usually connected. When I run, I write in my head. When I write, it's always about running. The exercise of writing and the feedback I get are deeply satisfying because I am able to connect with people in ways that would be difficult for me verbally. If I write well, it is because I am not the best of speakers. For now, I'll keep my promise. I'll keep looking for the one thing that pulls me and the few things I do well out from under my rock and into the fray of humanity. Though at times it is challenging, as I imagine it is for most of us, I still believe in myself, at least as a runner and a writer. I am thankful for that, for without that faith I'd be screwed.

I did figure out one thing. I remember the exact location the day I did, a nondescript part of the Bon Tempe Lake trail, climbing upward over twisting redwood roots. It was a perfect late-summer afternoon, warm in the sun but cool in the shade. My work was done for the day, and I had two hours of sunlight left to cruise the quiet trail around the lake. My legs were snappy, the breathing was right, and the time was good. It was easy. I had flow and full sync between my body and my surroundings. I thought, *I could do this forever.*

And there it was like sudden gold in my pan. I am going to run twenty-four hours for charity at the New Year's One Day race at Crissy Field in San Francisco.

I went to bed that night dwelling on my new idea. I brushed my teeth with the same toothbrush, tossed the extra pillows on the floor as always, assumed the usual belly-down sleep position, and almost fell asleep. But not before realizing I had gone through this exact same routine for—how long? And if I was going to carry out this new idea, it would be necessary for me to make a change. Our routines are all fine and good until they strap us down and keep us from following our ideas. To define is to sometimes make a change.

This need we all have to be recognized—I've yet to meet a person who wants to be completely ignored—is revealing. Here I was planning to execute this new definition of myself in a public realm. In my mind, that made it more real, more authentic, to have other people witness the thing I would do. We want others to know who we are. I could write and never put it into a book, but I do. I could run and never race, but I do. You could never put another political bumper sticker on your car, never raise your hand, never introduce yourself, never wear a SF Giants cap, but you do.

I remember the first time I did this defining business.

Downtown San Francisco 1979, cords and Cutlass Supremes. Weekday afternoon, that magic sunny hour after school and before homework. A ten-year-old kid named Alex, the shy one, running lap after lap on an elevated rubber-surfaced track ringing a gymnasium like an elliptical loft. Sometimes after school I would go to the Olympic Club with friends to swim, play basketball, or attempt to lift weights. But bored with games and the endless horseplay of boys, I decided one afternoon to run three miles, sixty-seven and a half laps on that mini track, just to see if I could. As I ran my steady pace, other boys would jump in, sprint fast enough to lap me once and then return to the court when their interest waned or they were out of breath. I watched an entire basketball game transpire below me as I swept around the banked turns. I outlasted grown men who had neither the time nor the desire to run endless circles. Lights started to flicker on and off, the club near closing time. I finished my three miles drenched in sweat. As I changed into my street clothes back in the locker room, one kid asked, "What were you doing up there?"

"I ran three miles."

"Yeah, right!" he said.

What was so hard to believe about that? I guess I should have known people would have to take my word for it. I had no witnesses from start to finish. I ran the distance not only to prove to myself I could but also to see what people's reactions would be. My running was an experiment, a call for attention. When the result was laid out, it was met with doubt. I knew most kids at that age didn't run that far, but I didn't expect disbelief.

Looking back, I wonder why I chose running to define myself. I could have been emulating my grandfather, though he was much more dedicated to golf and auto racing than running.

And I missed watching him in his running prime during the early seventies. I was too far behind to follow in his footsteps.

It was a moment in time I grabbed. I did it because no one else was on that track. While other boys proved their worth on the basketball court or in the weight room, I started running. It felt epic, almost like I was a soldier proving my worth for the battlefield. I wanted to be noticed, to be heard, to be told "you are worthy." That empty track called to me, told me running could be my voice. The disbelief I was met with after the three miles only galvanized running as my means of expression. *You don't believe me? Well, let me prove you wrong.* Looking back, I was mostly proud of myself for not letting an opportunity for me to be strong pass by. I wasn't always so good at seizing the moment. The trick is to be ready for the catalyst when it arrives.

So what was it about 1979 and 1987 that got me to reach out and grab and not worry so much if it turned out good or bad? Youth is the easy answer. But looking deeper, it was more than "ignorance is bliss." Instead of hanging out in the hypothetical world of my head, the land of what ifs, I spent less time back then asking myself questions and more time just doing, answering those questions in the way I ran: scraping my knees, feeling thirsty, finding a groove, getting my feet wet, falling down, getting lost, sweating on indoor tracks, finishing. When I got the idea to run New Year's, I had stopped looking so hard and was doing what I didn't have to negotiate with myself to do. No *If I run now I will work harder later*. It was just running for running's sake. I am happier when I am moving. Not running leaves me feeling anxious, not because it is something I have to do but because it something I think I am *supposed* to do. When I don't run, I feel that I am letting someone down, someone other than myself.

When I run, it is 1987 again. I can embrace difficulty and change. I can move with just a faint promise of something better simply because it is different. I can embrace moments instead of letting them slip away. Whether on trail or road, each run is an opportunity to create something on the fly. Free from practical distractions I am free to follow my desires—climb a mountain, jog down a street I have never been down before, race through a forest, splash through a creek, or stop to read a forgotten plaque on a city street corner. Running reminds me that moments can be made. For me, experience—not thinking, not pondering, not hypothesizing, not assuming, not adding to your to-do list—is the path to truth. Each run gets me a little closer to me as I move toward those things that are important to me, finding they are not as far away or as impossible as I thought they were. I grew up thinking a marathon was impossible. It's not, with some hard work. When I run, the question "What do I want?" is answered. Experience itself becomes the peak.

Less in my head, more in my body.

Less blaming others, more finding my own path.

Less guessing, more doing.

It's good to be deliberate. For me, there will always be meaning in everything.

Sometimes it feels like you should separate yourself;

sometimes it feels like you have to identify who you belong with. It's a lifelong task, this figuring ourselves out. And no easy task at that, waiting for the cream to rise to the top, shaking the strainer, whittling the wood. We're in there somewhere. I've always liked having two names. Alex is my practical name, what everyone calls me, who I'm known as. But Alexander is my goal, what's printed on my race bibs, and how I sign all my writing. Alexander is what I'm whittling down to. Someday, that's what you'll call me.

Do we stop changing when we find ourselves? I have a chronic redefinition problem. I can't settle into that one thing. Film school, teacher, carpenter, coach—the list will go on, I guarantee it. The minute someone tries to peg one of those monikers on me, I start to change. My grandfather owned the same business for forty-five years. He's always loved golf and auto racing. He's a steady guy and people love him. Me, I'm all over the map. What's with all the change in character? Why do I want to switch it up right before everyone figures me out? What am I running from or to? Maybe I am testing other people's endurance and patience as much as my own to see how long they will last with who I am.

Some dreams were ok to dispense with. I never really wanted to be an architect. But I am a runner now—again—and in that pursuit I am living a dream. I also remember that when I was a young man, I wanted to be a writer. I tried my best while writing this book to not forget that again. There are other ideas in my book of dreams. I've added a few recently. I'd like to travel the country in my truck. I'd like to write a really great running novel. I'd like to run a marathon when I am seventy. When my last day comes, I hope to cross off the last entry because I got up and did it.

No unfinished business.

Heads Up

I should have known better than to run in San Francisco at five o'clock, so close to dinner yet so far from home. Every restaurant in the city prepares their dishes at that hour, savory scents emanating from each establishment like a kind of invisible yet very effective billboard—Szechuan, Sicilian, Oaxacan. I didn't think I was hungry, but when bombarded by those temptations, my appetite rose to the occasion. Chinatown was a hodgepodge of garlic, earthy greens and pan-fried chicken. Across the street in North Beach, garlic still ruled, but was mixed with sweet tomato. Half a mile down Columbus Street, I ran through the steam rising from vats of boiling crab.

    I abandoned my planned route along the Embarcadero to begin a self-guided olfactory tour of San Francisco's dining options, following my nose wherever it led me. Hot dogs and mustard behind AT&T Park, BBQ ribs from a downtown smokehouse, fries from McDonald's. I stopped thinking about distance and route and focused on where I was and what I was experiencing at any given moment. Sketched out, my route would look like the pencil scribble of a toddler. I ran by hosts with menus in hand and by the loud crackle of meats sizzling in oil escaping from kitchen doors in alleys. My decision on which way to go was determined by what I could see and smell a block ahead. It wasn't until I found myself among the closed lunch-only eateries of the Financial District that I headed back to my car seven miles away.

Being one of the few times on a run when I was able to live in the moment made that afternoon significant. I didn't care how far I was going, whether it was up or down, fast or slow. I just relished the smells and sights around me, my enjoyment tied to the action of moving through these sensations. While living in the present is the gold standard, I find it hard to do. Maybe 5 percent of my runs achieve this state. Much of the time I'm either escaping the past (shortcomings as a younger runner) or preoccupied with the future (the necessity of a hard workout before a marathon). I rob myself of the present to pay for unresolved issues of times gone by and times to come, times I have no control over.

My best running moments are when I am just Alex, running through the forest or down the road. The breathing is right, the legs feel good, and I love where I am. There's no need to imagine anything else, no need to be in greener pastures. The act of running, a movement that is so instinctive and so satisfying, feels as right to me as a good night's sleep or a glass of cold water. I love it so much, it is hard for me to understand why many runners purposely distract themselves from the beauty of the act by running to music.

I once had an iPod addiction, feeling as if the little device was as essential as my shoes. Admittedly, running to the *Rocky* theme makes me faster. And that would be great if faster were my only goal. As much as I love it, each run starts to feel the same with music filling every void. Take away the sound of your feet landing on different surfaces, of the conversation of passing cyclists, of seagulls fighting over scraps, and replace it with the same eighty-eight songs, and you've traded serendipity for routine. No wonder we need running magazines' motivational issues. Disconnected from the anchor of ambient sound, it was as if I was watching a movie of myself running, a viewer rather than an actor. I want to be more than a member of the audience in the film that is me. Just as no two moments are the same, no two runs are the same unless we make them that way.

I've written about being lost in thought on runs, of how many of my best ideas come to me when I'm out on the trail. But if given the choice, I would rather dwell solidly in the moments I run, embracing the beauty of the act I love, thankful and appreciative of each step I take. I love running because it lays bare the one thing that is rightfully ours, which is not material goods or talent or motivation or even each other. The only thing that we really have is this moment, right now.

And our hunger.

And if we're lucky, a hot plate of spaghetti Bolognese.

The next morning was still black when I pulled my

truck into the gravel parking lot at Bear Valley in Point Reyes. Mistakenly, I thought the sky would show some signs of light at 5:45, but I had underestimated the length of night deep into November. So I waited, alone in the quiet dark, without even a scavenging raccoon to keep me company.

I was deep into training for the twenty-four hour race. With an extra long run ahead of me, I was anxious to start. My warm-up stretches were out of the way; my hydration pack was strapped to my back; my truck was locked; and I was just waiting for the sun to rise. 6:21. I went for it, knowing the first three miles traveled a wide dirt road that was easy to navigate even if I couldn't see where my feet were landing. But running in the dark transforms the silhouettes of familiar objects into primal fears. A huckleberry bush becomes a crouching mountain lion, a tree trunk the body of a stalker, a branch in the road a snake. *Ok sun, anytime now.*

I emerged from the cover of the forest onto Divide Meadow, and just like a dimmer switch slid up, the sky had transformed from the navy of night into the lavender of dawn. A wispy mist hovered over the grass two hours before the warmth of the day would pull it upward into dissipation. I told myself I made the right decision to run early. This wasn't a scene I saw every day. Furthermore, it took enduring a measure of uncomfortableness to get there. That seemed like an accomplishment in itself.

As I climbed to the top of Inverness Ridge, slanted square patches of yellow sunlight dotted the forest floor, illuminating swatches of our early winter's first green grasses.

The angle of light cast tiny shadows of each blade onto surrounding blades, all interlaced with the sparkling of dew drops. Normally I wouldn't notice this kind of detail on a run, but the fractured light called attention to the beauty of new growth. At the top of the climb, I was met with a blast of light as the sun beamed through the trees like a spotlight. I stopped running to look back across the valley. The purple blanket of dawn was pulled back like covers by the orange wash of the rising sun. The day had arrived. Light changes everything.

I could feel my mood lift as the morning light presented all that was ahead of me for the day. Now I could see distant valleys and ridges and perhaps, through the trees, the blue expanse of the Pacific horizon. Ground birds dashed across the trail from the underbrush to snatch insects only they could see, feeding on creatures not yet warm enough to escape. My dark morning of trepidation was now a day of possibilities. Enough resting. Time to run.

I dropped off the ridge down toward the coastline, running along a creek headed in the same direction. As I veered north, the creek became Alamere Falls and plummeted over the cliff onto the beach below. I, on the other hand, ascended a bluff overlooking the ocean five hundred feet below and twenty-five miles into the horizon. A procession of waves rolled in my direction and broke in rumbling bass tones at the foot of the cliffs. A turkey vulture spiraled upward from the beach, riding a thermal with ease. Somehow, in late November, I began to sweat lightly as the temperature rose into the upper sixties.

All of this life and warmth and movement made me think about how living things grow. From grass seedlings to the oldest Douglas fir trees, sun and water are responsible. The sun makes storms in the sea, which rain fresh water on land. Life is sustained by this water and fed by the sun. Excess water in the form of creeks and rivers travels back to the ocean to return to the mix, and it all begins again. It's a nice tight system. I wondered how I fit in.

I was exhausted at mile nineteen. My brain wanted to make sense of what I was doing, to understand how running through this environment had anything to do with the energy gathered and used around me. Mix equal parts fatigue, hunger, and the isolation of a long trail run, and you get thoughts of the deep and sometimes psychedelic variety. *What am I doing? Where am I? Who am I?*

The last four miles of my route took me up shady Bear Valley. The temperature in the shadows was a perfect fifteen degrees cooler. The coolness was a relief to a body I still had to convince to run for another half an hour. I was done, spent, bumping up against the limits of my endurance for the day. My movement was not propulsion but rather momentum, like the water in Coast Creek tumbling gently beside me back to the sea. We just wanted to get back home. Our work was done.

The purpose of my long runs is to train my mind as much as my body, to be comfortably lost in the activity of running for several hours. So I let my mind wander, give it space to think a thought longer than the distractions of daily life allow. That day I let it dwell not only on how depleted of energy I was the last two hours of the run but also on all the energy evident around me. I thought about the sun. Everything I had that allowed me to run long came from the sun, from the food I ate to the clothes I wore to the gas that got me to the trailhead. Energy collected, energy spent. The story of our lives.

I feel grateful that I am part of the system of sun, water, and life. I appreciate what it allows me to do. But part of being appreciative is saying thank you. How am I to do that to the sun? No hippie pagan dances here. I can't show gratitude to something as untouchable as the sun.

Maybe the best way to show appreciation for any gift is to use it, and use it well. I don't want to be the kid who leaves the lights on, Dad yelling, "You're wasting electricity!" So with humility, I will slip into the system. I'll use the energy I was given until it is gone. Through my running, I'll reflect my appreciation for the opportunity and ability to run all day in a place so alive.

In gratitude, I offered my ragged body, laying in the grass at the trailhead unable to run another heavy step, dreaming only of a strawberry milkshake and a nap in the sun.

Who was listening? I don't know, but I said thank you for letting me be a part of it all.

All Night Long

The experiment I began on the Olympic Club track continued with the twenty-four hour race.

I find that having a new goal is very gratifying, so I guess that makes me goal-oriented. I like the ones I give myself that feel just out of reach. Before my first marathon I was truly concerned I would not be able to run 26.2 miles. Before the New Year's race I was equally concerned I would not be able to run either twenty-four hours or one hundred miles, the mileage goal I had set for myself. That was a healthy fear.

Running is a deconstructionist pursuit though, psychological walls and mental blocks come tumbling down.

"I can't run that fast."

"I can't run that far."

You can, if you keep running.

No one will tell you running is easy, not an elite marathoner or someone training for their first 5K. It is work mixed with discomfort and pain that can cloud the eventual benefits of clarity, fitness, and a sense of accomplishment. Running is also the setting aside of excuses when we choose difficulty for it's promise of future contentment. When we stick with running, we acknowledge hardship has a purpose, that just because something is hard doesn't mean it is bad. I love challenges, especially ones involving willpower and endurance. I drape them around my neck like chains.

Easy isn't always better. If it were, I wouldn't be a runner.

Was it epic, this running for a day? I'd like to say it was, but I very likely asked too much of this race. Life-changing events can't be preplanned, because preplanning is another way of saying you put your guard up, believing you know all of life's threats, a know-it-all. But our lives are changed when that guard is down, when we're struck by something we never could have imagined, a threat to our status quo. That's when we see who we are by how we react. I had too long to mentally prepare for this race.

One friend said, "My husband said running one hundred miles is impossible, not that he would know. But, secretly, I thought it impossible too."

Friends and family were kind enough to keep their doubts to themselves in the days before the race. But just because you don't express a concern doesn't mean it goes away. Many people came out to Crissy Field to not only support me but also, I imagine, to witness the potential train wreck, accompanied by an inner shaking of their head and an unspoken *Yeah, I didn't think so.* I think some were there for the worst-case scenario to help pick up the pieces.

And it was a good thing that they were there, not because anything disastrous happened but because help was more valuable than I had anticipated. A lap race puts on a good display of a runner's ordeal. To have someone to talk to, to pour coffee when my hands were clumsy, yell encouragement, bring sandwiches, smile, confess to—these were some of the necessities of running for twenty-four hours that I hadn't considered. Luckily, I know great people, and they filled that need, stepping in to help as naturally as they would have tied their toddler's shoe.

This is my unedited race account from a voice recorder I carried:

Before 9:00 a.m. start - It's a beautiful day. I feel the need to pray, so I don't know if that's a good sign or a bad sign. Orange sun coming up on the way over. Clear. Pretty nervous, to be expected. Let's get going.

11:00 a.m. (thirteen miles) - All this talk of all the scenery in Crissy Field, and all I'm really doing is looking right ten feet in front of me. But, uh, I think the scenery will be more inspiring. Super clear day, shadows on the cliffs of the Marin Headlands. Clear as I look out to the west. But I am a little more tired than I thought I'd be two hours into the run.

11:15 a.m. (fifteen miles) - First visitor, Joe McGee,

my grandfather. Which is fitting—he was there at the start of everything. My daughter, Daniela, ran a lap with me. Perfect pacing. One-twelfth of the way done. Oh my God! No fractions.

Noon (twenty miles) - Staring at that bridge. I'm a runner *by* the bridge, runner *near* the bridge, not quite a runner *on* the bridge . . . yet.

There are people who are walking this whole thing. Can't quite figure that out. I'll ask them around midnight what their motivation is. There's a guy with gold sparkly Converse high-tops. I think I need to talk to that guy. There's another guy running, or rather walking, along with bushy gray hair. He's got an American River 50 Mile Race jacket on, circa 1982. He's got pants on, I think. No pretense of running, he's like a ghost of his former self. He's kind of freaking me out. Distractions are key. Can't wait until friends start to show up to run with.

12:30 p.m. (twenty-three miles) - Oh yeah, this is New Year's Eve. Surreality has begun. Starting to lose sense of time but I know it's 12:30. Almost twenty-three laps. Caught my shadow at the west end and I looked like Ron Cey or Bill Russell, 1970s L.A. Dodgers feathered hair.

7:00 p.m. (fifty-one miles) - Seven o'clock and then they were gone. I just had a steady stream of visitors, lots of people, it was . . . it just definitely helped with the last, um, six hours go by. Now sitting on a stool, looking at the bridge, about to eat my dinner of a turkey sandwich, banana, and Gatorade. Legs are super tired, a little tight. But I'm warm now and it's cool. No big epiphanies quite yet, but the night is young.

9:00 p.m. (sixty-two miles) - I just had a good two hour spell. I figured out that I was running too slow, actually. I was tightening up. Running faster was actually easier. And I was wondering where that came from. Was that you Chris Funk?

10:30 p.m. (sixty-six miles) - Just saw UFOs. One, two, three. One left. Now there's two. All right, and, uh, I know what I was going to say but I forgot . . . oh, I know this, uh, I know what's going to happen. I figured it out, epiphany time. So you don't know, but you will know by the end of . . . by the end . . . we're all looking at UFOs . . . and you'll know by the end of this entry. I just need to get to eighty, that's the plan.

11:30 p.m. (sixty-nine miles) - Just when I think I am out of this race and ready to walk the rest of it, I kind of . . . rise up. There's a . . . I think Chris is messing around with me. I want Brandi [Chris's wife] to know that people love her and want to do everything they can to help her, including doing crazy things like this. Maybe that bit of truth is more valuable than the money I'll give her for her charity, Headrush.

12:40 a.m. (seventy-two miles) - I have eight hours and twenty minutes to run twenty-eight miles. It's doable. Crazy that I'm considering that that's a challenge. That's just two more miles than a marathon, which I usually do in three hours. Wacky.

1:30 a.m. (seventy-six miles) - Got my routine down: Four laps hard, one lap cool down, stop, sit, eat, one lap warm-up, repeat.

2:30 a.m. (eighty miles) - My friends Kenji and Krause just showed up with some chicken noodle soup from Susan. It was the best chicken noodle soup in the world. Earlier I had the best oranges in the world. I've also had the best cookies, bananas, coffee, and water in the world. In this state, everything is now the best in the world.

3:00 a.m. (eighty-two miles) - My body feels beat up. Even my brain feels beat up from focusing on this one task for so long. I'm having trouble thinking straight about anything else than one hundred miles.

4:00 a.m. (eighty-six miles) - I just saw a poodle on the course. No wait, that was another runner's hairy legs lit up by my headlamp.

5:30 a.m. (ninety-one miles) - For the second time, I almost fell asleep in the Porta-Potti.

7:00 a.m. (ninety-six miles) - There's this older guy named Rocket whose been plugging along the whole time. I just ran by him and he said, "There he goes, like a metronome. Jesus almighty!" Ah, new friends. He doesn't realize I'm the same guy when I'm bunched up in sweats walking a slow lap every hour. To that guy he says, with a pat on the back, "You're doing great."

8:00 a.m. (ninety-nine miles) - Ninety-four laps equals ninety-nine and three quarter miles. That means I have to do ninety five. I ran a quarter of a mile and there was a stop sign. Ok. I made allusions to a surprise, to a plan, to an epiphany. Back in October, I decided I was going to run home after the event as a symbolic gesture. "Of what?" you ask. It had something to do with the desire I think we all have to create and be in a place where we are safe. My epiphany was that if I only made it to eighty miles, I could run the twenty miles home for an even one hundred.

8:30 a.m. (one hundred miles) - I had decided at 2:00 a.m. that I was going to stop at one hundred miles no matter the time. Done.

It was a good bit of hubris to believe I could run a hundred miles for the first time and then simply tack on another twenty. What was I thinking? At the end I felt an exhaustion deeper than I ever felt in my forty-two years of living. By eight thirty-five, I was asleep in the best sleeping bag in the world.

When the sun came up Sunday morning and I thought back to all of the family and friends that came out to help me, I knew I didn't travel those hundred miles alone. They fed me, held my hoodie up for me, slapped me high fives, walked with me, ran with me, stayed up in the night, pulled for me, and left me voicemails wanting to know how the story ended. I've never been good at asking for help when I need it, and that hasn't always served me well. But you know what? People like to help. People want to help. We've all felt the deep satisfaction of being there for someone. We don't need to look into it any further.

Later in the week, I kept thinking of circles, and not just the ones I wore into the gravel at Crissy Field. I was running to help Brandi's foundation, Headrush, and, in other ways, to lend Brandi a hand. Through pledges and physical support, I was helped by the people around me, which kept me going to help Brandi, which—you get the idea. The pull some may have felt to help me on New Year's Eve was the same pull I felt when I hatched the idea to run the race. If you see a need, and you know you can fill it, how can you not? It's fulfilling to feel a part of something meaningful, to feel you have a role.

Everyone who was at Crissy Field, in presence or in heart, lost someone too. I heard the stories. Brandi isn't the only one. There's been more to this whole

Headrush/twenty-four-hour endeavor than raising money. It's about us all seeing that we are not alone. Together we find the strength to carry on beyond a hundred miles, whatever our hardship. It ain't over.

So if home is where the heart is, then there at Crissy Field I didn't need to run another step.

"Here's the church, here's the steeple. Open the doors, see all the people."

I was acutely aware of all the people pulling for me to make it to one hundred miles, every last one of them as if an invisible electric thread connected us all. Sure, I could've walked out the door and run a hundred miles by myself. But I would have had my doubts, too. Never have I been more conscious of the web of people I am part of. Finally, I had found my own way to be in the service of others, as SI had asked.

But then, two months later, it was gone, that euphoric feeling of having done something right. It wasn't enough to look good in front of family and friends. I wanted more.

Yes, I ran for charity.

Yes, I ran a long way for a long time.

And?

I had thrown a Hail Mary pass to an unknown receiver.

I could tell you about the hallucinations, the massive calories consumed, the absurdity of trying to run two miles in an hour, but that's all trivia, facts without context. The truth is that I just ran for a long time in circles, and it hurt a lot, and that's all I really got out of it once the crowds were gone. A sense of accomplishment? Sure, I got that. I did what I set out to do. But I was waiting for that epiphany moment I assumed a race like that would produce, something beyond the show-offy maneuver of running twenty miles home.

I sugarcoated the venture in charity, which was a good thing I don't regret, because Headrush is a charity composed of friends. But it masked my motivations. I was trying to impress in much the same way that I did as a kid on the Olympic Club track—to look like a man standing alone. Who was I trying to impress? I think of how the two people who raised me reacted to what I did.

I have a lasting memory of my grandfather playing sentinel alongside the course, standing silently with his hands deep in his coat pockets, eyes behind thick glasses, watching me pass by every eight minutes. He didn't say a word, somehow knowing that that was the encouragement I needed. I don't fall for "way to go!" I need silent belief. I need steady presence. I need someone there.

My grandmother didn't come to the race, didn't even really give the event the time of day. If I had said to her, "Hey Grandma, I'm going to run for twenty-four hours," she'd have been pensive for a moment, chosen her words carefully while doodling in the margins of the newspaper, and then said, "Of course you will," understanding that I am as stubborn as I am athletic.

I wanted to make them proud, even at the age of forty-two. I think I did, but even that was unfulfilling in the end. How many more times must I beat my grandfather? And my grandmother? If I had the chance to ask her if the race was a good display of the direction she praised me for having, would she have voiced her approval or reminded me that I have a habit of punishing myself?

    I don't know. She died five months later.

Turnaround

I have found it to be true that there are two things you can't prepare for—the birth of a child and the death of a parent. I wasn't ready for the sudden and constant parental concern that came with the instant bond I felt the day I became a father. Though I am up for the task, the gravity of being responsible for someone's well-being is a weight I am still getting used to shouldering, knowing my actions and my words carry an exaggerated weight. The night my daughter was born, I felt irrevocably tied to her, as if an invisible tether bound us for our lifetimes.

In contrast, the night I got the news that my grandmother had died, I felt a tether snap. Maybe the tether is more fragile than I thought. Sure, I knew she was eighty. Sure, I knew she was in poor health, but things were rolling along. I was running strong and setting new PRs, writing a blog people were responding well to, coaching new teams, and feeling like

I was on my way to somewhere good even if I didn't know exactly where that good place was. Selfish as I was in my own pursuits, my grandmother's death didn't fit into my picture of momentum. The snap of the rope, the slamming of a book closed, the abrupt ending that death is, stopped me in my tracks with the pain of a new reality.

She wasn't just my grandmother. She was my mother figure. Standing in the street in front of 255 San Marcos Avenue, San Francisco in 1977, I cinematically waved goodbye to my mother and her boyfriend as they drove away, back to Los Angeles, leaving me in the care of my grandparents for the foreseeable future (forever, as it turned out). I stood in the middle of the street by myself with a dry and stoic look that was born that day.

Turn around, I begged my mom to myself, even though I knew it was hopeless. *Be strong*. I said to both of us. My grandmother waited for me in the house, angry at her daughter and concerned for her grandson. Moisture from a summer fog dripped off tall cypress trees to the patchy asphalt of the street, making puddles. The scene held the drama of a movie, the problem being I was in the movie. This was not LA, with palm trees and Santa Ana winds and skateboards and hibachi barbeques. This was SF, with fog and red steel, hidden stairways and geraniums, BMX bikes and jackets in August. Moving forward was a decision that was made for me. I was eight.

So it came as no surprise to me when, three days after my grandmother died and thirty-five years after I was first left there, I stood in the street in front of 255 San Marcos lamenting another important woman who was gone. I still wanted to be tied up in the knot of the family my grandparents and I had created. As much as I wanted to move forward, I wasn't ready to let go of my grandmother or that part of my history on Forest Hill. I wasn't sure how to. The house was gone, replaced by something newer. The Forest Hill neighborhood is all curved streets, hidden street signs, and dead ends. We never ordered anything to be delivered, because it took so long for the driver to find us, we could get it quicker by going out and getting it ourselves. This approach is, fittingly, a cornerstone of my personality.

Running is a natural outlet for my emotions. If I am happy or down or angry or relieved to the point where I don't know how to act on those emotions, I always find myself running. It's a physical expression of how I am feeling. Anticipating this outcome, I had brought running gear to Forest Hill. I started a run with the intention of revisiting all of the places I remembered spending time with my grandmother. I raced down 9th Avenue, past the House of Piroshki where she'd double-park so I could run in and get a greasy chicken, spinach, and cheese. When I arrived at the Golden Gate Park concourse, I found the patch of grass that she had found one afternoon so I could do my homework in the sunshine. She gave me a turkey sandwich wrapped in white paper, prepared with mayo and pepper. I didn't ask for it that way, but it tasted good. She knew. But now I had no appetite, just a desire to sleep. It was foggy. I closed my eyes.

I awoke twenty minutes later with nothing but a catnap accomplished. I continued running down the length of the park, up the steep incline past the Cliff House to Land's End. Striding along a path above the ocean, I eventually found myself in the Sea Cliff neighborhood where my grandmother once ran/walked for exercise. Was it the fog-obscured views or the lack of human connection that left my emotions empty? My run through the past wasn't anything but a flip through a book I had read a million times, chapters as boring as clichés. When I reached the second house we lived in across town at 16th Avenue and Lake Street, I stopped running. This farewell tour wasn't working.

It's so easy to tell people to be strong. As a coach, I work to establish trust so I can ask runners to do something they haven't done before, like hill repeats. I need them to believe me when I tell them "You can do it," so they can make the attempt and feel strong afterward. In this way, I am not giving them strength; I am helping them to bring it out themselves. What I hope to give them is the ability to see all the best things that I see in them. Good coaches address shortcomings but don't dwell on them. We want their displays of strength.

If only I could take my own advice. There are times I am so preoccupied with helping others feel strong that I neglect to turn the mirror on myself. Some say we despise in others what we don't like about ourselves.

Standing at 16th and Lake Street, I didn't feel strong enough to move forward. I knew I had it in me, I just couldn't summon it forth. So I took it down to the most basic level and ran back across the city faster than I had any business going. 10K pace, 5K pace, mile pace, exercising my physical strength to run fast and forward, to sweat it out, bullying my way toward calmer seas. I liked the work, but it didn't help much. I arrived back at San Marcos to an empty neighborhood, house gone, spaces cleared, just the same fog dripping from the same trees. Everything else I could picture from my recollections of that place was gone. In the last year, even my grandmother's memory started to go.

Reluctantly, I got back in my truck and drove out of that maze of a neighborhood. An approaching car flagged me down right about in the same place I last saw my mother that day thirty-five years earlier when she left me in my grandparents' care.

"Do you know where San Marcos Avenue is?"

I told myself I wanted to move forward. That seemed like the respectable and honorable thing to do. But in my own quiet Alexander way, I brooded, contemplated, analyzed, hypothesized, and dwelled on the snapped tether until my soul took on a mind of its own and began to lead me down a different, more rugged path than the easy street I had been on. I would run that path hard. If this were true pain, I wanted to know it well, like I know the tangible pain of running hard. The easiest thing for any of us to do is sit on the couch. But we know to grow we must stretch, work, breakdown, and rebuild, sometimes in painful ways. Running taught me how to manage pain as a means to an end because being comfortable with pain is not a bad thing for a runner. Maybe I just wanted control in this time of upheaval, but I believed pain could serve a purpose, which was to keep me from feeling numb. I embraced running because the invited pain of a hard run felt like living when there was mortality all around me. I didn't want my grandmother to die, but she did. The deep feeling of loss I was left with showed me how much I loved her. That's what I was grabbing on to by holding the pain: my love for her. If I didn't care, I'd have tucked her away. But that's not me.

Inside, I had reached my turnaround point. Any more loss of connection to my past, whether it was the house I grew up in or the people I lived in there with, and I wouldn't have been able to be present in the present. The past is a puzzle to me. I need to know how the past shapes my life here and now in order to avoid living exclusively in the past. My grandmother would have been disappointed in my nostalgia, though. When I was young I asked her what the song "Reminiscing" meant. Her only reply was, "That's nothing. You don't need to bother with that." She tried to forget her painful past. She would have said to me now, "Have some confidence in your ability to move on, Alex. You'll be ok."

Turn your head, Alex. Burying my past would have been easy for me. But I couldn't do it. I was asking questions of the past like "Why is running so important to me?" and not getting answers that satisfied me. Maybe I was asking the wrong questions. Maybe I was asking the wrong people. To go forward I had to go back further, because hurt is unfinished business too.

I said to the driver still waiting for directions, "San Marcos is back there."

Late Game Trilogy

I. My grandmother was Filipino. She came of age during the Japanese occupation of the Philippines during World War II. Her father was a well-known writer on the Japanese list of political threats. But he died when my grandmother was thirteen, thus transforming the problem of an adversarial country into a problem of family survival. After retreating to the mountains to go into hiding, my grandmother's family was forced to return to Manila for food and safety from the lawlessness of the countryside. She was educated by the draconian hand of Japanese nuns, women ready to strike her fingers with a bamboo switch if she missed a note during her piano lesson. Ostensibly to better her situation, my great-grandmother married off her daughter to an American GI when the US liberated the Philippines, and the war was over. The marriage was a business deal, born from greed and the need to control, which made the physical abuse that followed for my grandmother, mother, and aunt unsurprising.

At nineteen, in a moment of bravery or desperation, my grandmother boarded a passenger boat in Manila with her two young daughters and voyaged thirty days across the Pacific to San Francisco, unbeknown to her now-estranged husband. After a night in San Francisco, they took a train to El Paso, Texas—why, I don't know. They lived in Texas for a year, my grandmother working, my mother and aunt going to school, all while hiding from the hurtful hand of my biological grandfather.

They might have gotten away with it had my grandmother's health held up. She had already battled malaria as a child, but this was much worse—cervical cancer. In need of an operation that would leave her bedridden and unable to care for her children, she must have felt that she had no choice but to put her daughters on a train to Maine to live with their father, who was now remarried. I don't believe my grandmother ever forgave herself, for even as a child, I could feel the pain of her regret when she got that far-off gaze when I asked about the time before I was born. A pattern of parents and their children seeking a lost connection, one that started with the early loss of her own father, was now starting to set in place.

This is the story of my grandmother that my mother told me when I was an adult. As a kid, I sensed a deep sadness, deeper than words can describe, in my grandmother when she was around my mother, but I didn't understand it. With my mother's recounting of events, I began to understand my grandmother's anguish, an angry, bitter, hopeless piece of scar tissue on her heart she felt was her own fault. My grandmother was no stranger to pain. Through her, I learned to be hard on myself. I found a poem recently that my grandmother had written in Spanish on Sheraton Hotel notepaper:

> Silence in the night
> and all is calm
> the muscles sleep
> the ambition rests.

What a weird race the Dipsea is. It starts, but it doesn't, as I watch waves of older runners use their handicapped head starts to hustle up the infamous steps ahead of those of us spectating at our own race. I am used to younger men running away from me, but wrinkly seventy-year-olds? For this reason, I had resisted the Dipsea, considering it a club race for elders. What chance did I have as an in shape forty-year-old to finish in the top thirty-five and garner a coveted black shirt? Not much chance, I figured, as I watched nearly five hundred runners start before me. But as a runner I am stubborn and arrogant. I don't want their head starts.

I'm at the beginning of my middle age, not quite old enough to see my race times decline but aware that I'm not getting any quicker. I am smart now. I know the value of rest to squeeze out another good race. I'm tight. I ache. I'm restless in a way I wasn't when I was younger, but I am not ready to give up.

Maybe as we reach middle age we look to grab a few souvenirs, memories of our vitality from our youth. I grabbed something I did a lot as a kid, running, and my new found athleticism has tempered the effects of aging during years when I might otherwise have become less physically fit, years I might have found hard to accept. When I run I feel young. When I feel young, I forget all of those big forty-something questions for a little while, such as where the next paycheck will come from or if I'm healthy or if there will be an earthquake tomorrow. It's just running, just moving.

On my way at last, I charged up the stony 671 Dipsea steps. My reserves felt intact, and the breathing was in check, so I kept the momentum going and fell into a steady rhythm of passing people. I felt an easy fluidity gliding down the first descent, Suicide, ignoring the threat of root and rock and trusting my feet would find safe purchase. Every gap that I needed to pass runners opened up at just the right time, as if an invisible hand gently brushed them aside. To say that the running was effortless would be exaggerating, but I was in the zone where I willed my body to do something, and it responded, no questions asked.

My game plan to crack the top thirty-five was to run strong up Dynamite and Hogsback, the two successive ascents up Mount Tamalpais that make up the bulk of the climbing. As I dug in up Dynamite, I could feel my momentum gaining, even uphill. The same kind hand that moved runners to the side now pushed—no—pulled me along. I had rhythm and momentum; I was riding a wave. This was my day until the wave crashed.

Halfway into the climb, a deep and undeniable fatigue washed over me. I should have known better. A few scratch runners passed by, and I could feel discouragement begin to seep in with the rising heat. Now I would pay the price for running full tilt from the start.

I tried to think about something, anything, other than the pain that shouted to be taken seriously. It was all I could think about, how each breath seared my lungs, how shaky my legs felt, how the sun stung my shoulders. I would have to live with this pain that wasn't going anywhere. But how?

Because of the design of this handicapped race, the runners I passed were older and slower. That got to me after a while not because I felt sorry for them but quite the opposite. Usually if I pass someone around my age in a race, I think they didn't train as hard or, arrogant as it may sound, that I am a better runner. But when I pass an older runner who is breathing hard, pumping their arms all over the place, and carrying their worn frame up the hill, I know it has nothing to do with a lack of effort on their part or talent on mine. We are the same runner on different parts of the age spectrum. I am passing what will be me in ten, twenty, thirty years. So instead of pity, I now feel admiration. These guys are showing me how it's done. "I am he as you are he as you are me and we are all together." John Lennon got it right.

    I reached the top of Hogsback at the same time as a gray-haired toiler. He was sweaty and breathing rough, dust clinging to his damp shirt. But he was also leaning forward, stubbornly pushing off with each step. With just two miles to the finish, he was the definition of finishing strong. I expected my "way to go" to go unanswered, but he came back with a "go get 'em." The tone in his voice was bossy and appreciative, as if he had done all he could, and now he was passing a baton to me to move further along in this human race.

    I want what he's got—grit. He's a no-excuses kind of guy. Will I be full of reasons not to race when I am out of my prime. Will I say, "I used to run," letting vanity keep me from toeing the line? Or will I recalibrate my gauge of what it means to be a good runner and stubbornly push on, breaking the law of diminished returns? Will I be persistent enough to persevere? I am readjusting my expectations of my future self. There is a secret these old timers know about running late in life: that there is treasure beyond PRs. What we find is up to us.

And I wanted to find something by the end of this 12K, so I got back to work, harder than before, knowing I was in the midst of creating yet another chapter of my story as an evolving runner. When I believe I am on the right path, the pain sits well. It felt like the work of living. I could quit or keep it moving, simple as that. I raced to the grassy top of Cardiac Hill, barely slowing down to dump a cup of water over my head. The final descent begins at the Swoop, a narrow single track down a brush-choked gulch. My left foot caught a rock and I went down fast and hard. Middle toe stinging and possibly broken, I rolled on the dirt and picked myself up, the symbolism of the act not lost on me. I fell. I got up. I was ok.

I floated down the mountain, letting gravity pull me to the beach at whatever speed my weight dictated. The steps, branches, rocks, and roots of Steep Ravine were but passing obstacles to dance over. This was more than running now, this was releasing. Finally. I dug for strength I suspected was somewhere deep inside me but waiting to be released, letting barriers fall on top of caution. Though my body hurt from the effort, to live with pain no longer scared me. It was hard to be brave when I was scared. Falling now felt acceptable, even part of the whole deal.

I charged up the last short climb, Insult. With one mile to go, I ducked into the final shortcut but got caught behind two slower runners with nowhere to pass. I stayed calm, carried on, and then saw another gap open. I dove in, made it.

My friend Tom and his son Otis called out my place at the Stiles, half a mile from the finish. "Thirty-seventh! Go!" Somehow I knew I'd be here in the middle of all the drama of needing to pass two runners at the end. There was just enough time. When I hopped down to the final stretch on Highway 1, I knew I could use my road speed at last. I passed thirty-sixth place right away and caught sight of thirty-fifth place in the distance. I emptied the cannon with the finish line in sight, my vision dark on the periphery, the cheering of the crowd lifting me the final fifty meters. The announcer said, "There's the happiest man in the world!" as I raised both hands, pointed to the sky, relished my Olympic moment, and then collapsed at the finish line, too exhausted to stand.

  Running allows us to feel young, and it is safe to say many of us don't want to get old. So we train hard and chase PRs to distract us from the effects of aging. But we all know that day is coming when, no matter what our heart wants, our body cannot cooperate. Our bodies will betray us. But that old man on the hill gave me comfort that there's reason to carry that weight. I have determination to chase medals and black shirts. He has determination to keep at the work of living his life. He is old and wise and passionate. My grandmother wrote this down on a small piece of paper:

> Do not go gentle into that good night,
> Old age should burn and rave at close of day;

> Rage, rage against the dying of the light.
> Dylan Thomas

The Dipsea rewards runners who didn't give up, in that race or in their running career. Age is on public display. There is no instructional manual on how to get old well, so I observe and take notes. At the end of the day, I've learned that exercising your resolve is rarely a bad thing.

I stood on the podium with thirty-four other runners, male and female, ages eleven to seventy-two. It usually feels selfish or egotistical to say you are proud of yourself, but it felt ok to feel that way that Sunday. I discovered I was stronger than I thought. For an hour of our lives we refused to quit. Even more, we took the hard road and punished our lungs and legs in pursuit of a higher goal—to feel proud of ourselves for seeing it through. Maybe I'll negative split this running life.

Just three weeks earlier my grandmother had died, and it still felt as though I had lost her the night before. I didn't want to get stuck in the mire of grieving. It felt dangerous. I needed a hand, even a metaphorical one, to pull me out, something to show me pain and loss is not the end. People come and go in our lives. There are moments when someone's presence feels like more than serendipity, more than a simple ray of light, like the old guy running up Hogsback. Pain is not the end, or he wouldn't have been there. Nor would I have been.

II. I used to park my Hot Wheels and Tonka trucks under my new sister's crib. I used to watch the Apple Records label spin around while the Beatles sang of clowns gathered around. I used to walk the three long, straight blocks to second grade at Nativity Catholic School, careful not to break my mother's back.

But yelling between my parents turned into hitting. Marijuana turned into heroin. The cute bungalow on Amapola Street in a quaint neighborhood in Torrance turned into a bland one-bedroom apartment on Carson Boulevard. My father turned into just another guy when I was told one morning at breakfast that he wasn't my real father.

I visited my grandparents in San Francisco at the end of the summer of 1977. I never went home.

The morning of the Marin Ultra Challenge 50K was typical for a Bay Area summer day—foggy, fifty-nine degrees, and perfect for running. Waiting on the start line with about a hundred other runners, I sized up my competition and tried to determine who would be a threat. Casual jokes among one another, supposed relaxation, a little bit of nonchalance—these are the games we play.

The race started with a stiff two-mile, seven-hundred-foot climb up an old military road on the rugged coast. The strategizing continued as I doled my effort out in measured doses, a small push to show I was a contender but not so much that I'd look like a fool for going out too fast, too early. My primary focus was on the other runners, not so much the landscape. By mile fourteen, I was holding on to fourth place after the longest major climb. Constantly looking over my shoulder or spying ahead to catch glimpses of other runners, I maintained my position as we started to string out on a single track in the chaparral. Keeping my mind on my training and what I knew I was capable of, I methodically adjusted my pace based on the numbers my watch dictated. Halfway into the race was no time to get excited and push the pace. This was civilized, gentlemanly running.

Though I didn't know it at the time, I passed the last runner I would see for the day at mile nineteen for third place. I ran alone for the last thirteen miles. The fog had dissipated into summer heat inland. As I descended into damp Redwood Valley and saw the fog still sticking to the coast in the distance, I was thankful to be heading back in a westerly direction toward cooler temperatures. Deep fatigue was creeping in. My stride was getting shorter. This race was about to sing a different song. Lizards scurried out of my way, startled deer bounded into the trees, and rabbits who found themselves in the wrong place at the wrong time scampered back into the brush. We all ran as we always have. As toddlers, we learned to run mere months after learning to walk. Then it was always running, from point A to point B, until we were admonished to "Walk!" poolside or in school hallways. But now I was back to that natural state where ancient humans ran lightly between destinations. As I plowed through dew-laden grasses, I fell into a rhythm long forgotten. A difficult rhythm, to be sure, but one that felt raw and primal and natural in its challenge. Step by step, I drove my legs along the faint path and reveled in a motion uniquely human. The core of long distance running is rhythm and drive, not fits and starts. A melody in harmony with your surroundings. I left the scientific part of me behind. A vision lay ahead. *You are this song.*

The running felt so right I wouldn't have cared if another runner passed me. In fact, I would have patted them on the back for a job well done. Part of me missed running with someone. I like hearing other runners breathe hard with me. It lets me know we're in this together.

I doubt migrating birds or whales dwell on the distance they must travel. It's just the beating of wings and the slapping of tails to them, yet they travel halfway around the planet. The world to me became big and small at once. Small, in that I measured my progress in footsteps, big, in that I was fully aware I was three deep and narrow valleys away from my destination and the climbs that came along with them.

There I was expressing my endurance, though I was alone. This is who I am, who we are, and this is how I respond to being tested physically. And if the point of expression is to be heard, then the degree to which I am understood is how honestly I run. There is an old Super 8 film of me running in my grandparents' front yard when I was three. Before I was capable of giving it meaning, of asking myself why, I just ran, back and forth along a terrace built of cobblestones, stopping at each end to point to something in the blue sky. Without words to describe what I saw, I jabbed at the air to make my point. When that didn't work, I ran another length of yard. My running was an exclamation point. I had something to say, but chose my stride instead of my voice.

Descending the last quarter of a mile to the finish line, I heard the celebratory rattle of cowbells rung by race staff. Folks cheered me on as I cruised down the finish chute in third place. The array of food in the finishers' tent, spectators gathered, and the wilderness setting conjured up images of hunters returning to villages after a multiday hunt. Their return was celebrated with cheers and music and embracing—for the food they brought back, for survival, for a job well done.

And here we are. As I shook hands with fellow runners, smiled, and shared stories of the race, I felt for sure we had done this before.

> III. The narrative of my real father's absence, as succinctly told by my mother and grandmother, went something like this: He left when I was a year and a half old. He lives in Washington State on Lopez Island. And no, we don't hear from him.
>
> "I don't know how you can just not want to see your child," my mother said, without a hint of irony.
>
> "We used to argue about religion," my

grandmother said, conceding he was a smart man. "But you don't go looking for your father," she said when I expressed curiosity. "Children shouldn't seek out their parents. That's not right. If he wants to see you, then he can come to you."

Looking back, I understand their pain and disdain. They had been damaged by men. The problem was that was their story, not mine. So this dark figure became a dark cloud that I ran from. I got accustomed to reciting the same old lines to curious people that asked to be filled in. "I have never met my father. I live with my grandparents. No, I don't care."

Say something false long enough and you can almost start to believe it.

It took a new acquaintance, someone who heard between the lines I repeated without emotion, to be the first to say, "You need to let your father tell his story."

The idea stopped me in my tracks. It was true. I had only heard one narrative—my grandmother and my mother's story. But if I write for others to understand me, I should be willing to listen to others. It seemed only fair. Deep in the rhythm of embracing pain to navigate loss, I felt open to the possibility of getting hurt for the possibility of gaining someone I never truly ignored.

I reflected on times I ran until my lungs burned and on races so bad I wanted to quit running all together. I thought about gravitating to running as a kid, and then stepping away for many years, only to find the sport again when my overweight body needed it the most. I thought about the one day I went out for high school cross-country and the coach told me "It's not going to happen," feeling anew the sting of not being believed in.

In running I learned to believe in myself and, in doing so, was taught how to believe in others, which I had had a hard time doing after my parents left me. But in my earnestness to be strong, to be fast, to be epic, to be respected, I was calling out to the one I thought I would never see. The one I never thought I could believe in, no matter how hard I ran.

No, not God but my own father.

Faith showed me the things I believe in my head can be real in my hands. I learned that just the simple act of doing something makes more things possible than doing nothing at all, and saying that something is impossible and mixing that with inaction is a sure way of making sure it never happens. I can have an idea and put it into play. It might be ugly, but it makes for a life full of experiences instead of theories. I started to wonder if I could extend that kind of faith to other problematic parts of my life. Because up until I became a runner, I thought I would never meet my father. It felt impossible. I didn't believe in him. And I didn't think I had it in me. That's where my faith in myself ran out. But as a kid, I also thought running the New York City Marathon was impossible.

I'm sorry Grandma, I am going to seek him out.

After the family went through my recently deceased grandmother's belongings, they asked me to take a truckload of bags to the dump. One of her shoes fell out of a bag as I tossed it into the pit at the dump. I felt trashed, like I wanted to jump in there too.

I needed to run, quick. Like an animal released from a cage, I ran hard from my house to the Deer Park trailhead, trying to go as high as I could go as fast as I could. I didn't tell anyone, but the East Peak of Mount Tamalpais was my destination, no matter that it was 7:00 p.m. They'd all say I was crazy. Days prior had been windy. The worker at the stables commented on how many rattlesnakes were on the trails, some even striking at horses. Maybe it was all a bit reckless.

The wind was strong and relentless, easily gusting over 30 mph and creating a racket in the trees. While sometimes pushing me up and sometimes pulling me down the trail, the wind carried the scent of early summer's dry grass. I saw my first snake, a motionless garter, uncoiled and likely asleep. Still, a snake is a snake so I gave him a wide berth. But he couldn't have cared less.

I charged up Eldridge Grade, dancing over rocks that would like to twist my ankle. A few more snakes were on the periphery, possibly rattlers. I didn't stop to look, just avoided confrontation by running large arcs around them. The number of snakes was alarming, but so far my luck was good. Halfway up, the road gets rocky and bumpy, so it's important to pick your line. Though vague and difficult to see, the line is there, worn into the road by trail runners who climbed Mount Tamalpais before me.

Racing through the parking lot just below the top, I caught my first view of the peak up close. It was just a third of a mile push up a ragged boardwalk, and then a rocky stair sprint to the East Peak lookout tower. Nobody else was around. The mountain was all mine.

But a mere quarter mile from my destination, the largest coiled rattler I've ever witnessed squared off with me in the middle of the single-track trail. Heavy brush on either side made it impossible to go around. This couldn't be my turnaround. I had come so far. I negotiated with myself as to how much risk I would take on for the reward of making it to the top.

The rattler and I stared at each other for almost five minutes. Neither of us moved. With only body language to communicate, I decided to keep up a steady pace as I approached to show him I wasn't a threat, but indeed, I would be passing by. Ever so slightly, he straightened himself from his head to six inches down his body. I read it as an invitation: "You're cool, go ahead." Slowly and steadily, I walked toward him and rested my foot not a hand's width from his diamond head. His black tongue came out to flick at my shoe. Deeming me acceptable, he lowered his head back to the resting position. The hunger and cold were affecting my thoughts, causing me to almost reach out to him, but I thought better than to push my luck.

    I was as high as I could go at the peak. From the top of Mount Tamalpais, I could see what my life was so clearly. To the south lay San Francisco, the city where I was raised, all white buildings wrapped in blue bay, a city of dreams. To the north, in a nook of a forested valley, was my little town of Fairfax, where some of those dreams came true, while others were put on hold. Looking down, every part of the Bay Area fit so well together, like a puzzle finally solved. Thinking of myself down there, I felt for the first time that someone was watching over me, putting some people in and taking others out right when I started to take it all for granted. I decided right then to stop trying to control my future, letting go of the notion that I had it all figured out. Weather, the death of a loved one, natural disasters, a cramp at mile twenty-five—plans were for fools.

    I grabbed a boulder to steady myself as I stared at the Pacific Ocean while the wind ripped into me. I wasn't afraid of being blown down, or of the swaying power line, or of hypothermia, or of anything else in that moment. After my grandmother died, I was no longer afraid of death. For a moment in my life, I wasn't scared to live it.

However, I would have to pass the rattler again on the way back down. At the point on the trail where I last saw him, though, he was nowhere to be found. I looked, searching well in the bushes and, for some dumb reason, even flipped over a few rocks. Nowhere. Like he never existed.

Like he never existed. Like I put him there myself. Like I took him away myself too.

I ran back down the peak faster than I've ever run. As I cut through the parking lot at the top, I thought there would be someone around but it was empty. Just as I was about to duck down the trail at the far end of the lot, I heard the park ranger closing the gate for the evening. He looked stumped when he saw me across the empty lot.

"How'd you get up here?" he shouted from afar.

"I got here by running."

War is Over

"Nothing turns out as expected."—Michael Porter, my father

And this from a builder, a follower of plans. What did you expect?

It's typical for me that I had to attach something like a marathon to meeting my father for the first time. I couldn't just go see him. I had to put it in bold and underline it because it is a blessing and a curse that I must ascribe meaning to every choice I make and everything I do, not able to even pick what color underwear to put on without believing it will have an effect on the weather. Some people rightly call this superstition, reaching for control when we have none.

On the eve of the Santa Barbara Marathon, I imagined sitting on the beach and basking in Indian summer sun, swimming as the sun set in the cold Pacific. I would return to a nice motel room, saunter out for a little dinner, then kick back and watch some meaningless TV, ready to conquer the world come morning. That's what I expected. That was my plan.

But that November it was breezy and cool in Southern California. On the beach it was downright windy. The city felt deserted, summer fun seekers back to their daily grind in their hometowns. The motel room was tired, all rough towels and wall heaters that didn't work. I ate takeout soup from a little Styrofoam container and fell asleep early, unsatisfied and unfulfilled that the day before my big race felt bland. I had been feeling more nervous than I admitted to myself. But I felt no comfort from the little things that usually ease my worries. I wished the soup had been hotter.

My habit is to set high expectations for myself, then cling to them for dear life. The words my grandmother wrote to me in 1987, when I was 18 years old, echo in my head: "There are two areas of you that worry me. First, you are a little too hard on yourself sometimes. Ease up—it is vital for survival. Second, your well-known stubbornness. Try to be more flexible." I stubbornly wanted to bring a PR to my father, delivered like a freshly killed buck slung around my shoulders. But had I recalled her words on the start line, I could have guessed my marathon wouldn't have turned out as expected. As the stage for my running battle presented a different scene, I should have known the struggle had changed. I was hunting for something I had already caught.

> *"Being stubborn—well, there are principles, those are good to stick to. But then there is just wanting*

things your way and not accepting other possibilities."—**Michael Porter**

Everything went as planned at the Santa Barbara Marathon until mile eighteen, at which point I slammed into the proverbial wall like I never have before. I stared in disbelief as my watch read the increasing mile splits: 6:25, 6:43, 6:53, 7:05, 8:05. *Damn!* Running way over my head in pursuit of something epic, by mile twenty my sub-three-hour marathon was history. I started to walk, which was something I had never done in a marathon. I had no fight left in me to run. In fact, in that moment I decided that was the last marathon I was going to do. Something in me felt done and relieved to be walking at mile twenty. What I didn't feel was defeat, because it dawned on me that I was gaining something more valuable than a PR. One race does not determine if I am a runner or not. It was about the running, not the time. More to the point, it was about *being* a runner. As runners, our strength is not speed. It is endurance. Running or walking, I had no intention of giving up until I caught up to what I was chasing. In those last eight miles, I solved a mystery. It's important to know what you are hunting.

I have never known my father. Forty-two years ago he and my mother split up. My stepfather, Tom, adopted me, and until I was seven, I thought he was my real father. My mom told me the truth one morning at breakfast before school after they had split up too—that Tom was not my birth father. Time for school. Have a nice day. As I moved in with my grandparents, I never looked back, fine with my father being the big mystery in my life. My grandmother stubbornly stuck to her line that children should never go in search of their parents. I was young at the time, so I believed her.

But in the absence of a father, I ran to prove my manhood. I have not had the benefit of having the male half-responsible for me being in the world teach me how to be a man, and then have the opportunity to push him away and assert my own identity. I never wanted to push my grandfather away. I was too aware of his sacrifice. I was too thankful. I needed my father before I realized it, and that need didn't fade with his absence but only went awry and manifested itself in unnatural endeavors like running marathons to fill the void. Marathon after marathon, I tried to prove my worth to an unknown entity until I was so deep into it, I couldn't see that I ran my body into the ground in Santa Barbara, couldn't see the establishing of myself was complete no matter if I gained a PR or not, couldn't see the simplicity of the one more thing I had to do until I stopped trying so hard.

When my friend convinced me to meet my father, they reminded me that I had made choices, namely running, to define Alexander. I had already addressed my fear of being the same as him by choosing to define myself outside of his influence. If the picture of my life is a series of small brush stroke choices, I can look back to that urge to run, not just as a little boy but also as a thirty-nine-year-old man, as dabs of paint of a self portrait on a mostly blank canvas. They were decisions to move on my own, at my own speed, and in my own direction. With this in mind, I could handle all of the similarities with my father I would come to discover—from the fact that we both are builders that drive white trucks to that he once ran and played drums and that we both stand the same way for pictures with one hand on our hip—because I had chosen to do all these things without him. Maybe his unintended gift was to force me to be independent from him before I even knew his name. Maybe.

I have been chasing my father. With him now in my sights, walking became acceptable. So while in Santa Barbara I gave in to fatigue at mile twenty and walked, I never gave up on moving forward. In fact, I feel like I won because I was finally able to reach him. If I were still looking back at my past to figure it out, I was doing so over my shoulder and with one foot in the future. I walked across that finish line fatigued and in pain, put that medal around my neck, and then dragged my weary body to the ocean for a swim. It felt right to surrender to the moment and stop running, even if it was scary. I'd done all I could do, so what more was there to do? I wanted to be something and I became that. Runner, definition complete.

The surname I was born with was Porter. I was Alexander Sebastian Porter. And what does a porter do but carry other people's bags? With time to grab on to what can still be, it was the moment for me to let go of what should have been because nothing turns out as expected.

By sunset of marathon day, I was driving east on I-10 through a desert landscape not toward home but to Arizona to meet my father. If this was my true race, I had him in sight. The race was coming to an end. Usually the desert would frighten me. I've never liked it much. It doesn't feel like a place people belong in. But in its austerity, it's beauty, its openness, I could breathe in the orange glow. I felt ok. I could feel us coming together as the distance shrunk between us.

Though I was filled with confidence and resolution, there was still a surreality to my task as I drove through the desert to do something I swore I'd never do. It was like I was trying on a different me. I gripped the steering wheel of my truck and thought about what it would have been like to have grown up with just my father—if he would have shown me how to build or if he would have disappeared into a book, if he would have played catch or claimed sports were a waste of time, if this was a drive I would have made during the holidays. I had my grandfather, but he was my catcher in the rye. What would it have been like to have grown up his responsibility for better or for worse?

I stayed the night in a characterless chain motel in Mesa. He lived east in Apache Junction, about twenty-six miles away. At the end of the road toward his home loomed Superstition Mountain, which was fitting because this day was about confronting things I didn't understand and making sense of mysteries in my life. For so long I had imagined our first meeting to be different. My old worry was that my grandmother, my father's mother, would die before I met my father for the first time, and that I would be forced to meet him at her memorial under circumstances beyond my control. My plan was to be preemptive, taking a train up to the Puget Sound to introduce myself on my own terms.

So many times this movie played in my head: I walk down a forested road with a piece of paper in my hand bearing his address. Three miles later I stand at a dirt driveway, the number painted on the post matching the one scribbled on the note. In the distance I see a parked flatbed truck beside stacks of firewood. As I walk on to the property, I notice a small house hidden by the trees that separate it from the road. Its design is simple, its shingles unpainted and dark like the forest that surrounded it. Scattered about the surrounding land are half-built carpentry projects still in progress.

A light wisp of smoke rises from the stone chimney of the house. I step up to the door and knock. No one answers. But I hear the sound of a man struggling somewhere in the distance. I walk across a patch of wild grass and fallen leaves toward the sound on the edge of the forest. From the trees comes a man dragging a tree stump with a rope, his back to me. He moans and grunts with each tug as the stump's roots get tangled in a network of undergrowth. I watch the man walk backward toward me.

"Do you need a hand?" I ask.

The man spins around startled. He has a beard the color of a cedar tree that extends down to his chest. His unkempt sandy-brown hair is mixed with silver. He lowers his eyebrows as he starts to realize who I am. For a brief second I have the sensation I am looking into a mirror.

"Do you know who I am?" I say.

He nods yes.

"She brought us together in the end." I say, regret in my voice.

But this day couldn't have felt any different. No forest, no busy man, no surprises. I felt a certainty in my trajectory, as if my path had been illuminated and I could see my way, as if someone had whispered to me that I would end up here all along. What choice did I have now but to own the moment? I marched up to his doorbell with purpose. If this were a movie, I would have paused with my finger on the doorbell, flash back to years of mystery, take a deep breath, and push the button nervously. Surprisingly, I felt no hesitation or fear, only resignation about the task I had set for myself. I feel my strongest the day after a marathon because I know I did something hard, and I am all right. I remind myself over and over again of what I have done. It gives me confidence. Standing on my father's front steps tired and achy and sore from running, I rang the doorbell, confident I could take on more difficulty if need be. I had summoned him. It would only be seconds before I presented my weary-runner self to my father. Those were my last fatherless moments. Those were my last moments on my own.

A truth that has been hard to admit to anyone though because of my pride and ego is that, ever since I learned that Tom was my stepfather, I have thought a lot about my father. I played it cool, and I played it tough when his name came up in conversation. But when no one was looking, I would sneak a peek at the few pictures I had of him, studying the color of his beard and wondering what he was thinking at that moment. I told people that it didn't bother me that I didn't know him, and then, subtly, through roundabout conversations with my mother, I would glean bits of his story without her knowing what I was doing. I lionized him by imagining him to be a master builder of craftsman homes, an intellectual who deserved to smoke the pipe I saw him holding in one photograph, a kind and gentle soul who missed his son but was too embarrassed to admit it to his new wife. When no one was looking, I studied the handwriting and meaning of the only words he ever sent to me in my youth, an inscription on the inside of a paperback copy of *The Lion, the Witch, and the Wardrobe*: "Just thought I'd let you know I still think about you." I wanted to believe he was a truthful person. And what did he think about when he thought about me?

    One thing I do believe is that whether you love or hate your parents, whether you know them or not, whether they were good or bad to you, that in the end you cannot ignore the effect they have on your life, that everything we do in our lives as their children is in emulation or rejection of them. I believe this to be true because I have come to accept this about myself despite years of saying, "I have nothing to do with him." I have everything to do with him. The way I live my life as a man is a result of not knowing my father as a boy. Not knowing my father had always felt like a birthmark on my identity. It wasn't a birthmark, though; It was a bruise that healed and disappeared with patience, maturity and resolve.

    With that in mind, I felt true to myself to be standing on

Michael Porter's doorstep, seeking to end the mystery of who he was. I heard his footsteps behind the closed door. I was running for answers. I had arrived.

And there he was.

Early sixties, receding gray hair, short sleeves, strong and worn hands. This was no stranger. This was the man I studied in pictures, forty years later. Our first minutes together felt all too comfortable and familiar. Maybe he had thought about this day for a long time too. Our greeting was cordial and understated—reserved, as I am guessing is typical for both of us. He showed me his house in the desert, the masonry wall he had built that hurt his back, the cacti growing wild. He and his wife Twanette did well for themselves. There was an ease to how they moved around their home. But in my father's words I sensed a shy confidence. He was proud of the house and home he had built up, but he never thought he'd be justifying the merits of dry desert air over Pacific Northwest mist, especially to the son who experienced neither with him. There was a shakiness in his voice. But I liked it. It told me I meant something to him.

For lunch we ate clam chowder that Twanette had made. He remarked about my 141st placing at the marathon. He had looked it up. I was touched. I thought all I wanted to know was that I didn't come from a deadbeat dad, the one my mother and grandmother portrayed. But then he said, "That's pretty good." In that one comment, he removed the burden of heavy goals I'd set upon myself. He looked impressed. He was trying to connect with me. I was going to give him all the reasons why I didn't do better, like I still had something to prove. But I wasn't there to give him excuses.

I was there to present myself, my beat-up-but-still-standing-marathon self. I wanted him to see Alexander. He saw. He noticed. I didn't need to run—I needed those three words from him. "That's pretty good." I sat perfectly still at his dining room table, absorbing the words. He kept speaking about the marathon, but I wasn't listening that closely. I got all I ever wanted in my life from him in that split second. In every race I ran, I needed to be needed, to feel like I mattered. I wanted him to be proud of me. When the two most important people in your life leave you at an early age, it becomes your life goal to feel important. And I caught a glimpse on my visit to him of what I hoped was his need to need me. Whether we do anything about it or not, all of us parents need to know our children are ok. Did you eat? Are you warm enough? How was school today? I needed to feel like a son, even if just for a second. In return, I brought him a bond between father and son, slung over my shoulder, that circumstance and stubbornness did not sever.

"Yeah, not bad," I said.

We talked about each other's lives, about the past, about our families, blah, blah. I still wasn't listening. I was tripping out that I was talking to my father. He was humble, honest, and chose his words carefully. At the end of our morning, he showed me a half-built sailboat over twenty-five years in the making in his garage. He'd begun it on weekends on Lopez Island, Washington with his stepfather. He told me he hadn't finished it because he wants to wait until the time when he can do it right. I did the same thing in meeting him, waiting until it felt right. We're both guilty of having patience.

I asked him what he was going to name the boat.

"Jeri Lynn, after my stepdaughter."

Michael Porter wants to be a father. I want to be a father. I cherish my fatherhood of my daughter because, honestly, part of it is about me needing to be needed too. Did my father also feel his world was off-kilter not knowing me? Someday I will ask him. Maybe I am too forgiving, but I am happy Michael Porter got the chance to be a father, even if it wasn't with me, even if it was with another man's child. In fact, another man raised his child. He's right, things don't turn out as we plan them.

By the end of that evening, I was back on the Southern California coast at Redondo Beach, the last place I remembered being able to call two people mom and dad, even if that was an illusion that fell apart soon after. Back then I knew where I fell in the scheme of things. But since that morning at breakfast when my mother told me that Tom wasn't my father, I have been running for answers. If, like most children, I was egocentric, I also became aware on that day that big, powerful, painful, and joyful things happen in spite of you. There is so much more to the story than the one that is being played out before you. The whole story about my father and how I fit in—that's what I was running toward.

Sometimes my running provides too much introspection, long miles with the same deep conversations with myself. I had to get out of my head and into the real world—that was the Santa Barbara Marathon, that was the drive across Arizona. I place a high value on empirical knowledge. Just as I can't be a runner by watching the Olympics, I couldn't know my father without meeting him. I had to find out for myself, clear out my own dark cloud. Now I can say I know Michael Porter. I can even say I know him a little bit as my father. Cold-calling him one sunny but cool October afternoon was me tired of being a fatherless son, was me tired of fighting a battle I never signed up for, was me starting to write my own story and not the one others wrote for me, was me leaning at the tape at the finish line.

    That race is over. I can call myself a runner.

    Like runner, like son.

    There's still time to be young.

Dear Lola

Dear Lola,

    I still have it, the letter you wrote to me while I was on my Catholic-school retreat. The black ballpoint ink looks so fresh, like it was written yesterday. Your name stretches proudly across the letterhead in Futura font. Blanca. April 26, 1987. I always meant to write back to you. Is it too late now?

    I miss you.

    Do you remember the Super 8 footage that Lolo filmed of me in the front yard on San Marcos Avenue? I must have been about three, making a scene in my Ely Red Ball overalls as my mom and Tom looked on. Come to think of it, they mostly looked at each other, arm in arm, obviously in love. I raced back and forth on the terraces, maybe trying to get their attention, maybe doing my own thing, which was to run the length of the grass, stop abruptly, and point to the sky. "See what I see?" Then it was back to more running. Lolo must have been excited because the footage shakes. I bet he was laughing.

But you? You just stood and watched me like an owl—calm, plaintive, arms crossed, observant, choosing your moments. Something was on your mind—bigger things, deeper issues. But you didn't look worried. You looked tough and ready. Were you still mad at her for getting pregnant so young? Were you mad at yourself, thinking it was all your fault? Come to think of it, there were owls all around the house: little glass figurines, framed prints, tablecloths, ashtrays.

I think you had it figured out, long before anyone else did, that that's what I had to do, that running would be my way of expressing to the world the words that were hard for me to say. You were never impressed when I started running marathons or when I ran the twenty-four-hour race. If I had told you beforehand of my running plans, you would have said, "Of course you will."

I do think you were proud of me in your own way. You were proud I took it upon myself to take care of myself. In my earnestness, in my persistence, in my stubbornness, you knew I would be ok.

Lolo was generous and kind. How could he be expected to be hard on a boy from a broken home? That's why I am hard on myself, because who else would be? You told me about the expectations your mother had for you back in the Philippines when you were a girl. I learned all about the strength one needs to make one's parents proud.

In that footage, I didn't live with you yet. That would come in a few years. But when I was seven and it was time to leave you after a Christmas visit and return to Los Angeles, you felt in me the heavy sadness I tried to keep inside as I kept more quiet than usual while my mother loaded luggage into the front trunk of our yellow VW bug. It was a new sensation for me to feel longing for someone, to feel a love I couldn't comprehend the depth of yet still feel its weight. You offered me a spoonful of peanut butter as we said goodbye on the curb of San Marcos Avenue.

"But what about your spoon?" I asked.

"Keep it. You can give it back to me next time." My eyes got watery. You asked, "Are you ok?"

And with that I burst into tears, and my mom and Tom set me down gently, crying, on top of the extra suitcases in the back. Those were my first tears for another person. I knew the hurt the missing was about to bring. I buried my face in the back compartment, unable to watch you and the Forest Hill neighborhood get smaller in the tiny window out the back. I cried all the way to the 101.

Like an orchestra conductor, you guided me. You knew when to call me back in Sausalito. And you knew when to let me roam in Venice. I needed your voice of caring and trust to become strong on my own on the stage you set. I was a quiet kid. I didn't talk much. Somehow, you knew what to listen for, making me feel heard even when I didn't speak. That gave me confidence in my expression. You believing in me let me believe in myself. It gave me the strength to run.

Run, I did. When words fail me, running speaks from my heart.

I wrote this book to tell you how it's been since you've

been gone. It's been hard. Life feels like endless work.

You used to do this thing with your eyes where you'd raise both eyebrows twice in quick succession. You told me that was how Filipina women would convey "I get it" without saying as much. The very last time I saw you, laying on your bed the night before you died when I still thought everything would be ok, you did that thing with your eyes. I knew how you spoke too.

When you died it was hard to say good-bye not because you were gone but because I didn't know how. I wanted to. I knew I had to. I spoke at your memorial, chastising everyone for seeing you only as their cook. I went through boxes of photographs and letters you had left behind for me. But each gesture only highlighted your absence. I wish I could have given you this book, but it is too late.

So here is my gesture to make you proud of me one last time—I met my father. I ran the Santa Barbara Marathon, drove across dry California and dry Arizona right after and I did it, I met him as I think you always knew I would do. In ways I only see now, you were prepping me for it. You told me I would know when the time was right. And I did, forty-three years into my life and about six months after you died. I built up the strength, mostly through running, to meet him on my own terms. I had to be stubborn about that. You would be especially proud of that. You had to be stubborn as well. From the day he left, you knew my father wasn't coming back. You also knew I needed him because you needed your father too. You, who lost your father at such an early age, knew firsthand the loss that comes when a parent-child bond is in distress. In that Super 8 footage, you knew I ran back and forth to call out to the man who should have been in the picture. You let me shout, in my own quiet way.

So now that I know what you gave me, I can say thank you. I can also say good-bye.

I am ok.

Love,
Alexander

Alexander Sebastian is a runner, carpenter, coach and writer living in Northern California. Like Son *is his first published book.*

The back cover photograph is Superstition Mountain, Arizona.

The title font is in the handwriting of Blanca Guzman taken from personal letters.

www.ingramcontent.com/pod-product-compliance
Lightning Source LLC
Chambersburg PA
CBHW021955290426
44108CB00012B/1079